THE STORY OF A HOUSE

ASKHAM GRANGE WOMEN'S OPEN PRISON

EDITORS
BRIAN LEWIS
&
HARRY CREW

FOREWORD
HELENA KENNEDY QC

YORKSHIRE ART CIRCUS

IN ASSOCIATION WITH

ASKHAM GRANGE

1997

Published and distributed by
Yorkshire Art Circus, School Lane, Glasshoughton, Castleford, WF10 4QH, &
HMP Askham Grange, Askham Richard, YO2 3PT

© Text:	Yorkshire Art Circus & HM Prison Service
© Photographs:	The Askham Grange Collection and Central Office of Information
© Commissioned photos:	Stephen McClarence
© Cover image:	Jim Park
Cover design:	Paul Miller @ ergo design
General editors:	Frances Brett, Lorna Hey, Reini Schühle, Clare Conlon
Support team:	Harry Malkin, Sandra Hutchinson, Elizabeth Hargreaves
Design Team:	Reini Schühle and Brian Lewis
Typesetting:	Reini Schühle, Art Circus Education
Printing:	HM Prison Enterprise Services, Wellesley Road, Croydon CR9 3LY
ISBN:	1 898311 30 7

British Library cataloguing in Publication Data
A catalogue record for this book is available from the British Library.

This book, done in association with Askham Grange, is part of an arts-based community consultation programme which originated in the Yorkshire Art Circus.

Yorkshire Art Circus is a unique book publisher. We work to increase access to writing and publishing and to develop new models of practice for arts in the community. Please write to us for details of our full programme of workshops and our current book list.

Yorkshire Art Circus is a registered charity No 1007443.

Yorkshire Art Circus is supported by:
Yorkshire & Humberside Arts, West Yorkshire Grants, Wakefield MDC Leisure

Contents

Like all the best stories, the one contained within this book is many layered. It describes a beautiful house with a lively history. It introduces the occupants of old and those of today. Within this one story there are hundreds more, worthy of Scheherezade's collection of tales. They tell of human success and human suffering, hope as well as hopelessness.

There is always a special poignancy for me in hearing fragments from the lives and experiences of women prisoners and those who work with them. They invariably confirm me in my view that the majority of women who end up in prison should not be there at all. By and large they have committed offences of dishonesty - social security or cheque card fraud, shoplifting or handling. Increasingly their offending is linked to drug abuse. Many of them have suffered sexual abuse and violence in their own childhood. Most of them have been the victims of crime more often than offenders. They have done wrong but they are not wicked. What they need more than anything is help and incentive to put their lives together in a productive way.

It is hard to fathom why women who are not involved in violent offending, professional crime or indeed large scale dishonesty, should be so readily imprisoned. Recent research by the Probation Service suggests that more women than men go to prison for a first offence often because of the scarcity of alternative sentencing options - particularly if the woman cannot pay a fine or there is no suitable community service available for her. In a system designed essentially for men, women can reap the consequences of inadequate provision, unsuitable to their needs.

Another underlying problem, which too often remains unspoken, is that society views female offending differently. One of the main reasons why men commit crime is because it enhances their sense of masculinity, but the reverse is not true; far from it. Women who commit crime feel reduced as women by the process of criminalisation because they know they are perceived differently from their male counterparts. When women commit crime, they not only offend against the criminal code, they are seen to have breached sacred notions of what is deemed to be truly female. Those attitudes towards female offending seep into the criminal justice system, unconsciously affecting the sentencing process and leading, I suspect, to the inappropriate imprisonment of women.

The consequences on the lives of the women and their families are untold. Women's prisons are scattered over the country, often a long way from family and friends. While men can usually rely upon wives and lovers to remain supportive during their incarceration, men seem to find it harder to stay the course or to play that kind of role. Separation from her children is one of the most searing of losses for a female prisoner, endorsing her sense of failure as a woman, and profoundly affecting the children.

However, reforming the whole of the penal system is beyond the remit of this book. What Brian Lewis and Harry Crew draw together are the voices which evoke the spirit of Askham Grange and explain why it is such a special place.

Over the years many of my female clients have served time at Askham Grange and it has always been a source of relief when they were allocated a place there rather than in one of the larger institutions. The women acknowledged that while this smaller open prison was not a holiday camp, the ethos upon which it was founded encouraged rehabilitation, the acquiring of new skills and the sustaining of relationships with family and friends beyond the prison gates. They knew that they would be more than just a number there and it mattered to them.

We are living in a climate which is increasingly punitive towards those who have fallen from grace and committed crime. The call is for more imprisonment and tougher conditions. Prisoners are demonised and in the collective imagination seen as unlike the rest of us. The whole direction of penal policy is based upon retributive justice and all the knowledge we have gained about effective and successful ways of diverting offenders from crime are being abandoned.

Fortunately, enlightened pockets of good practice still exist. They succeed against the odds to maintain education programmes and therapeutic work for prisoners with little encouragement and inadequate resources. Askham Grange is one of those places. The story told in this book is more than the story of a house: it is the story of punishment's failure and the success of rehabilitation, it is all about human redemption and the ability to change. This is a story to be told and told again.

This is the story of a house which has had a varied history. When it was first built in 1886, it was the house of a Leeds factory owner; half way through its life it became a hospital and for the last fifty years it has been a very innovative women's prison.

The book has been structured to reflect the history of the house through its rooms and the voices which have echoed through them. This is a very natural structure. A house needs to be systematically built of stone, brick or concrete but it is a mean building if it does not contain embellishment in the form of decoration and social purpose. The chief embellishment of Askham Grange will always be the people who live inside its walls.

There is a saying, 'A house is a machine for living.' The interconnecting image of domesticity and engineering has always had great appeal to me so I was particularly intrigued by the description Harry Crew, the current governor, gave of his job:

> *I like to think I am a 'governor' in the engineering sense - balancing and regulating the separate elements, putting a little oil in here, taking a bit of heat away there so that all the parts function smoothly together.*

This book is therefore about the act of balancing: Balancing the needs of people who have been found guilty of crime but who deserve a chance to re-educate themselves, and the need of society to temporarily remove some citizens from normal freedom. We reflect this balance by letting people speak for themselves.

A number of people and books have helped us. Mary Baldwin is Askham's historian and she put at our disposal her excellent manuscript and her time. Two books were published in the early 1950s, one by Mary Size, the first governor, and another by a prisoner who calls herself Jean Henry. Both give lucid, compelling insights into the early years of the prison and

Instead of parking women in prison, I should like to imprison them in a park.

provide the historic context for our story. This story builds on the conversations we have had with prisoners, officers and friends of the prison. The writing was done partly by the people who told their story and partly by our team of writers. Where the writing reflects the past we dated it. All undated pieces take us up to the present and cover three years, from 1995 to 1997.

Some people were spoken to by design: The Chaplain, the Chairman of the Board of Visitors and the Senior Probation Officer but chance played a big part in the writing collected in this book. Whenever someone was available we sat and talked with them. If time had permitted it would have been wonderful to talk to everybody. We feel that everyone is represented and we would like to thank both the writers and the whole Askham Grange community. Team work creates the ethos of this community and makes it a positive force.

The cry that payment of a debt to society should be extracted in as brutal a manner as possible was heard in 1947 and is still heard, but the modern emphasis on rehabilitation rather than punishment received a boost when open prisons, including this one, were instituted following the Second World War.

1997 is the fiftieth anniversary of the Grange as a prison. Its philosophy is based on the idea that the purpose of custodial sentencing is to ensure that prisoners do not re-offend. This, rather than an eye-for-an-eye-and-a-tooth-for-a-tooth mentality, sustains the open prison movement: Open prisons are an alternative which is more efficient and humane.

Brian Lewis

'You cannot train people for freedom in conditions of captivity.'

Alexander Paterson,
Prison Commissioner
1922-46

Stephen McClarence

The Aims of the Askham Grange Prison Community

1. To care for every resident with tolerance and understanding, offering equality of opportunity and taking account of their right to personal dignity and privacy, whilst maintaining necessary security

2. To provide a quality of accommodation and furnishings that will enhance a sense of self-worth, but to be in keeping with constraints appropriate to the purpose of the residence

3. To develop positive relationships with the local and wider community and promote the principle of reparation through community and charity work performed by the residents of Askham Grange

4. To create purposeful living based on constructive and challenging activity in both work and leisure periods

We would like to thank a lot of people but especially the women prisoners and the officers. They have talked openly about their experiences and we are grateful for that.

Amanda	Angela	Ann	Bev	Carol
Charley	Claire	Diane	Dorothy	Emma
Geraldine	Gillian	Helen	Jackie	Jennifer
Jenny	Joyce	Julie	June	Kathy
Lynne	Kelly	Kim	Lhea	Louise
Lulu	Maggie	Margaret	Michelle	Paula
Pauline	Rachel	Sally	Sandra	Sarah
Shelly	Susan	Val	Wendy	Vicky
Wilma	Yasmin			

George Aitkin	Mary Baldwin	Sue Blackburn
Frances Brett	Barbara Britain	Jackie Brown
Carol Burke	Kay Cairns	Carol Carter
Roger Clegg	Glenis Cocker	Helen Crew
Jim Dawber	Kathryn Dodds	Matt Dodd
Judith Dunhill	Jenny Farley	Alexis Hanford
Elizabeth Hargreaves	Jo Henderson	Roger Henderson
Sandra Hutchinson	Linda Marmara	Rhona McMeekin
Margaret Middlemiss	Garry O'Reagan	Jim O'Shea
Debbie Palfreyman	Tony Parrish	Leslie Redpath
Andrea Richardson	Pat Rhodes	Reini Schühle
Stephanie Slater	Kathryn Stainburn	Carol Sturzaker
Wilfred Theakstone	Ann Thistleton	Sarah Wardley
Mary White	Carol Wood	David Wood

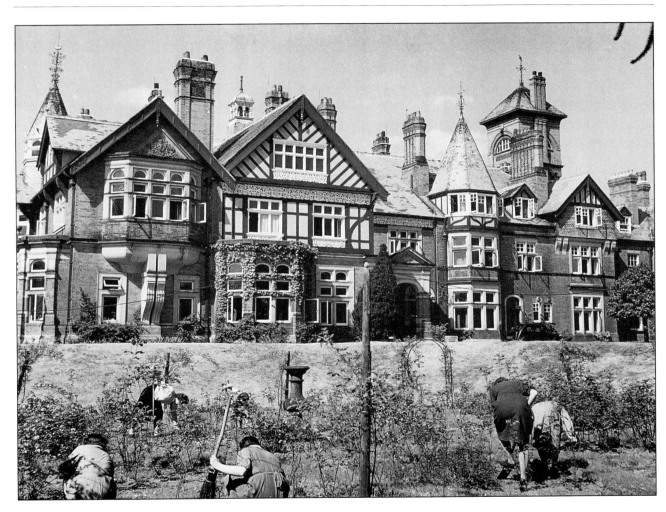

Stephen McClarence

A WOMEN'S OPEN PRISON

We must remember that inmates of penal establishments will return to the community sooner or later, and will sit beside us in the train, on the bus, at the films, or in the restaurant, with no bars between and no walls around them. Unless we have planted the seeds of self-respect, moral integrity, and a desire to become an asset instead of a liability to the State, we have not protected society from the criminal and we have failed in our mission.

Mary Size, Prisons I Have Known

MORE THAN BRICKS

A house is more than bricks and mortar, in the same way as the soul is more than the body that contains it. As you enter the village of Askham Richard, Askham Grange with its sky-reaching water-tower dominates; everything else is smaller. The main road leads to its gate. Toy houses and a duck-filled pond flank the way. On the green, a pump donated by the house's first owner offers 'drink and rest' to the weary traveller.

Beyond the wall encircling the Grange, the green changes to formal gardens with beds and pathways. Then you are inside the house itself: the panelled great hall, where three butlers once held sway; a fitting place for Major Wailes-Fairbairn (Squire, Soldier, and Big Game Hunter) to hang up his trophies. A corridor leads off, taking a sharp bend before the kitchens. The house had this ground plan so that domestic smells could be kept at bay; at least that was the theory. On the other side of the hall lies the 1914 wing, a ballroom above an oval swimming-pool, a twenty-first birthday present for the son of the house. Another passageway gives on to the new Mother and Baby Unit. And from the heart of the hall, a flight of steps leads to the stars: an arched window decorated with coloured zodiac signs.

'We are not inmates; that suggests that we are more than a bit crazy, we're definitely not clients or girls. Call us what we are: we are prisoners.'

Up a further flight of stairs a second hall opens out under a glass dome. Beneath this, a wooden balustrade surrounds three layers of reinforced glass, revealing the great hall below. Hallways branch off, showing room after room, one leading to the administration rooms. Higher still, stairs lead to the old servants' quarters.

Frances Brett

AN EDWARDIAN GRANGE 1914

The ballroom block was opened in 1914, and took three years to build. It was first opened with a ball for the gentry and the hunt people. That was on the Wednesday and on the Friday they gave a ball for the servants and staff. There was a fair number of staff in those days. There were three butlers, a footman and odd job man, a cook/housekeeper, kitchen maid, scullery maid, two housemaids, two laundry maids and a ladies maid; that was the staff in the house, indoors.

Wilfred Theakstone

PAINTED IN DELICATE PASTEL SHADES

The name Askham means the homestead near to the ash tree. *In the Old Norse language the ash was* askr *and* ham *is found in Early English and means dwelling place.*

The name Askham Grange had conjured up for me a rambling old country farmhouse with attending outbuildings and stables, adapted to serve its new purpose. I am bowled over by its stunning setting, and totally unprepared for its stately, oak-panelled interior. I viewed the ornate plaster garlands and cornices, all individually painted in delicate pastel shades, with wonder. Can this really be a prison - even an open one?

Elizabeth Hargreaves

GUIDING PRINCIPLES

The contrast between the big sign outside the prison close to the lilac trees and the one in Reception was really marked. The one outside threatened you with everything short of decapitation if you transgressed. Drawing teeth for the sheer fun of it was definitely on the cards if you as much as brought in a couple of cigarettes and left them for a prisoner to mind. By contrast, the sign inside Reception was humane and liberal. It reflected the first of the prison's Guiding Principles: *To care for every resident with tolerance and understanding, offering equality of opportunity and taking account of their right to personal dignity and privacy, whilst maintaining necessary security.* Serious stuff that.

Askham Grange must have looked similar when Mary Size took over in 1947. There have been changes: the billiard room is now the chapel, the dining room is purpose built at the other end of the house. There is a new education block but even so you see more similarity than difference.

Brian Lewis

ASKHAM GRANGE 1947

The mansion stands in ten acres of ground, with tennis courts, gardens, woodlands and lake. This area is fenced to divide it from the adjoining parkland. There was no entrance gate; it had been taken away and broken up during the war. A new wing as an addition to the original building was completed in 1913 or 1914, with the outside architecture in keeping with the original structure, though the interior was on modern lines.

On the ground floor is a large ballroom panelled in light oak, with a sprung oaken floor, and a stage at one end. Radiators are fixed on raised platforms on two sides of the room, and the beautiful carved oak pillars which

Mary Size had been the Assistant Governor of Holloway but had retired. In 1946 she was asked by the Prison Commissioners to come out of retirement and establish an open prison for women. Volunteers were called for to serve with her.

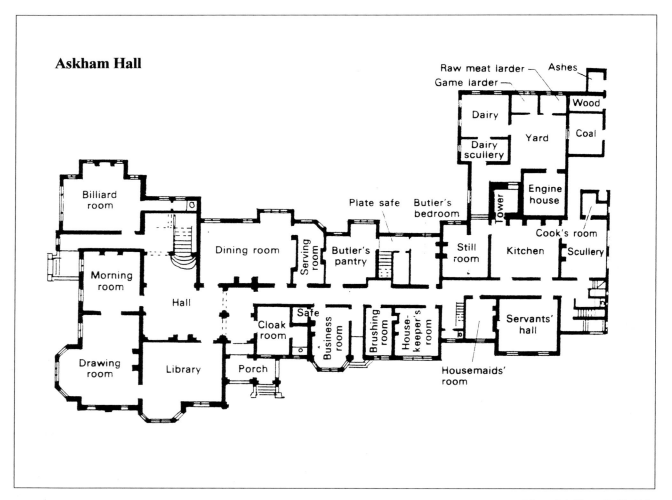

Askham Hall

Raw meat larder — Ashes
Game larder —
Dairy
Wood
Dairy scullery
Yard
Coal
Billiard room
Engine house
Tower
Cook's room
Plate safe
Butler's bedroom
Dining room
Serving room
Butler's pantry
Still room
Kitchen
Scullery
Morning room
Hall
Cloak room
Safe
Business room
Brushing room
House-keeper's room
Servants' hall
Drawing room
Library
Porch
Housemaids' room

Plan of Askham Hall, 1886

support the ceiling break the line of the platforms and give the impression of alcoves. A minstrels' gallery completes this room. The ceiling is in the ornate Italian style. The lighting is from crystal bowls suspended from the ceiling. Underneath this room is a swimming pool now used for storage.

On the floor above the ballroom is a suite of rooms, comprising four bedrooms, a reception room, two bathrooms, toilets and a small kitchen. The bedrooms and bathrooms are situated on either side of the corridor, and the reception room is at the end of the corridor over the stage. This is a lovely room with a very large bay window facing the door, and two other windows. It has an unusual ingle-nook with light, oak-panelled seating and a raised platform hearth with a basket grate. An attic, with two bedrooms and a bathroom, completes this new building.

The large entrance hall with a wide staircase is panelled in old English oak, incorporating a fireplace which had been removed from the manor house before its demolition. A radiator enclosed in oak panelling is under the main staircase, and one along the wall adjacent to the entrance door.

The library, a very large room with walls lined on two sides with mahogany bookshelves, opens off the hall. This room and the dining room are heated by open fires. The library, drawing room, morning room, billiard room and dining room open off the entrance hall, and the principal bedrooms are placed immediately above them on the first floor. A door opening from the hall to a passage is the entrance to another wing of the house on the ground floor, off which were the domestic offices. Adjoining the dining room is the serving room. This is followed in rotation by the butler's pantry, servants' sitting room, store room, and lastly the kitchen and scullery. On the other side of the passage is the estate agent's office, which opened off a little corridor leading to a side entrance to the house. Facing this is the gun room. Further along the main passage is the housekeeper's room, followed by a China store, and next to that the

Since Mary Size's days some of the rooms have changed their function. The library is now a conference room, the television room has moved into the former dining room. The butler's pantry has become a suite of cells. Prisoners now sleep in the original morning room and the ballroom is used for badminton and keep-fit.

Governor Size and staff, 1950

servants' hall. Immediately above this floor are bedrooms and bathrooms. The flat which had been occupied by the male servants was on the second floor, but had no communicating doors with the remainder of the wing; it has a separate staircase. The bedrooms are on the first and second floors, the top or attic floor being the women servants' quarters. Here then was Askham Grange as I found it in December, 1946.

Mary Size

GOVERNING PHILOSOPHIES

The governor's reports, from Mary Size's right up to Harry Crew's, give you a good idea of the philosophy which governed prison life. In the early days the plan seemed to be that the prison regime was to produce housewives and homemakers.

Strange when you think about it; these women governors were part of an early generation of career women yet needlework, painting and decorating were encouraged along with toy making, glove and slipper making and garment assembly. At the beginning of its history as a prison Askham was in a bit of a time warp. In the age of mass-produced clothes and synthetic fibres Askham Grange prisoners were encouraged in fine needle work and embroidery, the accomplishments of Victorian ladies rather than skills more appropriate for women who had spent the war years in munitions factories.

Governor Miss Mary Size, in very early reports, found it sad that out of the 28 women employed in the workroom making shirts for male prisoners, not one knew how to make a shirt. There wasn't much of an attempt at equipping women with skills other than crude repetitive ones. In 1948 the Askham Prison population was around the sixty mark; the workforce turned out 3590 shirts and 1000 green money bags for the Royal Mint.

Brian Lewis

The old house creates its own ghost culture. My two favourite spectres are the two gentlemen sons of a long dead owner: one is said to be called Brian and the other Richard. They walk through walls in evening dress and occasionally get exorcised.

A Brief History Of Askham

The present building was built by a Leeds firm of architects, Chorley and Connon, when Sir Andrew Fairbairn was 58 and his wife, Clara Frederica, a little younger. Sir Andrew had his finger in a lot of pies: He was an MP, a Captain in the Yorkshire Hussars, a Knight of Grace of the Order of St John of Jerusalem and vice-chairman of the Royal Albert Asylum, Lancaster. He also presided over the building of Leeds Grand Theatre in 1878. In every way Sir Andrew was influential in Leeds society. Politically he was a Liberal and for a time he occupied one of the country seats in the East Division of the West Riding. When that went in a redistribution, he held the Otley seat for a while. Then, following dismemberment of Gladstone's Party over the issue of Home Rule, he supported the Unionist faction and was subsequently defeated.

By religion an Anglican, Fairbairn had a degree from Cambridge, was called to the Bar in 1852 and had lived in America and Germany, but the bulk of his life had been spent at the centre of the commercial life of Leeds. In his middle years his deep interest in education and the public library movement led him to be on committees which planned Leeds Central Library and he was elected first chairman of the Leeds School Board. He was an active philanthropist. Though not in the same league as enlightened capitalists like Sir Titus Salt of Saltaire, he was nevertheless interested in active paternalism. It is said that he built St Mary's School because he could not bear to see the village children trudging across the field in all weathers to Askham Bryan. Its furnishings and fittings were well above the standard required by the Education Department and he provided a new house for the school mistress close to an excellent school building.

Sir Andrew died childless on 28 May 1901, and the estate passed to a nephew, Major W F Wailes, farmer and landowner. Joint Master of the

Askham Bryan comes from the Old Irish personal name Brianus, whereas Richard is likely to refer to either Richard Earl of Cornwall, or another thirteenth century Yorkshire lord, Richard Malebys de Askham.

York and Ainsty Hunt, he also was an ardent big game hunter who spent long periods of time abroad. He changed his name to Wailes-Fairbairn.

The fortunes of the family were following a pattern common in the nineteenth and early twentieth centuries. At the beginning there was an entrepreneur, Sir Peter Fairbairn, who put down the footings for a secure capitalist enterprise. His son, Sir Andrew, built on those foundations and became gentrified. The third generation, lacking either the iron will, hard work or imagination which established the fortune, adopts the habits of gentlemen, fails to build for its future, and starts a downslide which it is difficult to arrest. The buying of a country seat like the Grange, bringing as it must a divorce from urban roots, complicates matters further. Mergers were pushing the Fairbairn family and firm further from the centre of commercial power. As early as 1880, when Sir Andrew went to Parliament, managers and accountants were already taking over the company. An absentee tiger shooting squire ensured that by 1914 the influence the Fairbairns had in decision making at his factories was negligible.

However it was not financial failure which moved the house away from uncomplicated domesticity, but a world war. As soon as hostilities broke out in 1914, Major Wailes-Fairbairn, although 53 years at the time, volunteered and rejoined the army. With a husband and a son on active service - Neville W F Wailes-Fairbairn was a lieutenant in the Yorkshire Hussars - Mrs Wailes-Fairbairn turned Askham Grange into a convalescent home for wounded soldiers. An appropriate act, for on 20th July 1916 her husband was badly wounded.

After the war the house reverted back to a family dwelling but, after the death of Neville Wailes-Fairbairn in a hunting accident in 1939, at the onset of hostilities his widow handed the Grange over to the government on a fifteen year lease and moved into a converted stable in the Park.

Brian Lewis

This prison is committed absolutely to a policy of racial equality and the elimination of discrimination in all aspects of the work of the prison staff, it is opposed also to any display of racial prejudice either by word or conduct by any member of the service in her or his dealings with any other person.

Notice in the Entrance Hall

THE FIRST WORLD WAR 1914

It was the First World War that changed everything, after that nothing was the same again. I was nineteen when it broke out and went to enlist early on. I worked up to the Saturday night and started in the army on the Monday morning. I earned sixteen shillings a week in those days; poor money, but I was in work and that was what mattered. We accepted long hours starting at 6.30 in the morning and going on for almost twelve hours. On my reckoning I did a 58 hour week. If you were a cricketer and belonged to the cricket club you could reduce that by a couple of hours. Most things were hand done and needed a lot of individual attention.

The Grange provided work. In the garden, for instance, there was Charles Davies the head gardener, plus the foreman; the first, second and third journeyman and me. Everybody knew where they stood. Mind, this was only small compared with other places. Grimston Park had a garden staff of eighteen in those days. Then the war came and several of us - including Charles Davies, captain of the cricket team - did our duty and went to fight in France.

Wilfred Theakstone

THE HUNT BALL 1914

Northallerton grow mushrooms, and East Sutton Park make cheese for the commercial market. New Hall have a dairy herd and pigs. Our tomatoes go to Lindholme and are then distributed to different prisons.

When the time for the York and Ainsty Hunt Ball came along there was always a good deal of excitement. It was the custom that each evening the head gardener had to make a button hole and take it to the lady of the house so that she could wear it at dinner, but when the Hunt Ball was near the steady rhythms of the house changed and the Grange became a profusion of flowers. In those days they had a large garden staff, and the greenhouses.

There was no shortage of labour then and by the time the coaches, and later cars, started to arrive everything was ship shape and Bristol fashion. The lawns had been freshly cut and the gravel newly raked. Mr Fairbairn was always insistent that the wheel marks were gone as quickly as possible.

All the village was excited. Palms came in from all over the place and chairs were set on the balcony at the top of what was later called the Governor's Staircase. Then, when the party was in full swing, servants and villagers were let in and allowed to peep at the assembled company from a small grille above the ballroom.

Wilfred Theakstone

ASKHAM GRANGE *1949*

Askham Grange is for 'star' prisoners, first offenders, recommended for transfer to an open prison by the governors of the traditional prison to which they were committed by sentence of the court. They must be suitable for the special treatment and training in which places like Askham Grange specialize: Their term of imprisonment must run for at least another six months before their release so that they can profit from the 'open prison' technique.

This technique does not mean giving the prisoners a paradoxical freedom, as many emotional opponents of the open prison system assert. It means placing the emphasis on moral rehabilitation rather than punishment. It is an attempt to restore these girls and women to society as better people than they have been, not as hardened and embittered criminals such as often emerge from the ordinary prison to liberty and a life of continued crime.

Unknown Journalist

Any person who claims to have deep feelings for other human beings should think a long, long time before he votes to have others kept behind bars - caged. I am not saying there shouldn't be prisons, but there shouldn't be bars. Behind bars, you never reform, you will never forget. You never will get completely over the memory of the bars.

Malcolm X,
Autobiography

GOD FEARING CITIZENS 1947

When it was made known that Askham Grange would be used as an open prison for women, the inhabitants of Askham Richard became alarmed. That was the reaction to be expected from a small and peaceful community of law-abiding, God-fearing people. They had little sympathy with those who broke the law of the land by robbing, plundering and sometimes murdering decent citizens. It is understandable that they regarded such people as most undesirable neighbours.

Many of them had restless nights wondering what their fate might be when their beloved Grange, their squire's home, from which they had derived so many benefits in the past, was now to be the first prison without bars for women offenders. What protection could they hope for from the law breakers who could walk out of the Grange as easily as they themselves could walk out of their houses? The thought was frightening and haunted some of them day and night.

Their attitude towards the staff at the beginning was not hostile, but it was easy to sense a feeling of fear cloaked by a reserved manner. They did not make friends with us easily. Like many other people, they probably thought that prison officers were chosen for their work because they were cruel, coarse and hardhearted, and therefore not nice people to know.

We took the first step to break down their reserve by trying to show them that we too were hard-working, God-fearing citizens, trying to do a job of work with which they happened to be unfamiliar. We attended their whist drives in the village hall and sometimes provided prizes. We took an interest in their social activities and tried to make them understand that we would be prepared to help. Slowly their fear and resentment lessened and a wholesome and genuine friendship developed.

Mary Size

This was the first women's open prison. East Sutton Park in Kent was opened in October 1946 as an open Borstal Institution for girls. Askham was for adults.

MORTGAGES 1955 - 1995

The village and the prison were closer forty years ago for the simple reason that both governors and officers lived in the village, drank in the pub and got involved in a very practical way in parish affairs. Now, to all intents and purposes, it's a nine until five job. Governors and officers try to work with the village but although there is a will to be involved most staff live in houses that might be twenty miles from the prison gates. Some will say that the trouble is that the prison has become more isolated because its regime is more liberal. Maybe that's the case but the main reason for the village and prison not knitting together as they did forty years ago is a change in the way we all live these days. We are not settled any more in the way we were then.

Of course it's not one-sided. We have people in Askham Richard today who commute to Bradford and a lot who work in Leeds. Village life itself has changed.

Mary Baldwin

ASKHAM GRANGE 1991

When I first arrived there was still an upstairs/downstairs mentality. Prison officers still called the women 'girls'. There was nothing seriously wrong with the staff, but not much money had been spent. It felt very neglected. I gave the decorators the freedom to be expressive, allowed officers to choose colours - people were free to use their imagination. I obtained money and spent some of it on pictures to lift the spirits. I was anxious to liven up the place making it a good place in which to work, live and learn. Recently we have changed the Gate into a pleasant Reception area with curtains sewn in the education block.

A day in prison on which one does not weep is a day on which one's heart is hard, not a day on which one's heart is happy.

Oscar Wilde,
De Profundis

Stephen McClarence

Governor Harry Crew, 1996

Women prisoners like a place to be tidy and fresh. They don't abuse the space in the way men would. The panelling in the main lobby wouldn't last ten minutes in the average men's prison, it would be covered with graffiti. Yet, although I wanted to make the best of what we had, I didn't want to seem to go over the top.

Askham Grange feels like a National Trust house so it does demand a certain approach. My difficulty is not to overdo it. What standards to have? How much to decorate? I aspire to a good guest house, not a five-star hotel.

Harry Crew

GOING INSIDE YOURSELF

You can see faces and stars in the plaster at the top of the main stairs, right up on the ceiling. They're not immediately obvious - it's not what you expect - so I wouldn't have seen them at all if someone hadn't pointed them out to me when I first arrived here. I'd stopped looking for detail and beauty.

When I first came here, a year ago, I was amazed. I'd seen the house on the telly before, but when I actually came here, I couldn't believe it - it was so beautiful. I was walking around, looking at every little thing. I loved the window with all the star signs in it. But then I began to shut off. You have to do that when you're first here, to keep your privacy. Some end up doing it all the time. The only space that's a little private is your room, but you share that. So you end up going inside yourself. And you have to do it because you can't keep thinking about the outside world. You'd go mad if you did. You can't sort anything out from in here. If you've got problems outside, it's best to leave them there. Some women spend all their time

There is no graffiti in the toilets, though you sometimes get a bit in the bedrooms.

Graffiti is not part of this prison's culture, and any graffiti is dealt with immediately.

Harry Crew

worrying about what their bloke's doing: Who's he with? Who's he seeing? You can't deal with all that. It will all be waiting for you when you get out anyway. You just have to forget it for the time being and keep your energies for in here. You find a bit of this place and try to make it your own. Last summer I spent ages, especially at weekends, under the dome, staring up at it, trying to work out the pictures on it. It's really dirty, so it's not easy to see what they are. It nearly turned into a habit; I wasted so much time staring at it that I don't go as much now, though sometimes I still go and look.

I'm not saying I don't think about home. I think about it all the time: Part of my mind is always somewhere else, going on ahead.

Prisoner

MY NEXT BEDROOM

Colours get me started. In my mind I have done out my bedroom with a dark grey ceiling with spot lights, white cornices and also a picture rail. The wall is a lighter grey and I've sanded and varnished the floor. I had the radiator cabinets built with criss-crossed woodwork which conceals them but lets through the heat. There is a *his* and *hers* wardrobe built around a fireplace; this is pure white with elegant brass fittings. My friend makes curtains and she made these with tie-backs that hook on to big brass hooks. Furniture is sparse. There is a king-size bed with a picture at the head framed in brass flecked with black dots. The windows are leaded. There are two white bedside lights, great big white fluffy cushions on the bed, and white fluffy rugs.

Prisoner

I know not whether laws be right
Or whether laws be wrong;
All that we know who lie in gaol
Is that the wall is strong;
And that each day is like a year,
A year whose days are long.

Oscar Wilde,
The Ballad of Reading Gaol 1898

SUBJUDICE

All over the Grange there are phrases in Latin; what people make of them is anybody's guess. When he retired, storeman John Leech made a list, photocopied it and passed it to anybody who wanted a copy.

Omnia Bona Bonis	- To the good everything is good
Qui docet Discit	- Who teaches, learns
Subjudice	- Under consideration
Omnia Vincit Labor	- Work overcomes all difficulties
Servato Fidem	- Keep your promise
Par Oneri	- Equal to the burden
Justitiae Sorror I Fides	- Trust is the sister of justice
Vive, Vale	- Live and farewell
Ne Cede Arduis	- Don't give in to difficulties
Finem Respice	- Look to the outcome
Quantum Libet	- As far as it is possible
Veritas Odium Parit	- The truth causes hate
Vincit Quise Vincit	- They win, who control themselves
Ex Uno Disce Omnes	- From one learn all
Vide Et Gredere	- See and go on
Utile Dulce	- Useful and pleasant
Vita Brevis Ars Longa	- Life is short, skill is everlasting
Omnia Vincit Amor	- Love conquers everything
Satis Verborum	- Enough of words
Suus Cuique Mos	- Each to their own taste

Nana Mansah, my grandmother, said to me when I was a child, 'Learn to aim high and be somebody, Ghana is now an independent country.' So I did a range of subjects at school; economics, mathematics, health sciences and the study of my own language, which is Twi. Schooling was good.

Prisoner 1995

I ONCE PERFORMED IN LEEDS TOWN HALL

My dad was a blacksmith and for entertainment in the pub he would bend an iron bar around his neck. His neck width was about nineteen to twenty inches. Sometimes he would pick my mother up whilst she was sitting on a chair. She weighed about fourteen stone. I can pick a chair up with my teeth.

I had an excellent run at middle school, played the trumpet and flute, played netball, got A's in all my exams and took part in the school production of *Singing Samson*. We performed it at the Leeds Town Hall to over a thousand people. It was a rock musical and I played instruments and sang a solo piece. I've always stood out wherever I go.

I changed when I got to High School. Now it was smoking behind the bike sheds, bunking off, but no one seemed to be bothered whether I turned up for lessons or not. There was no one there to explain that education was important.

Prisoner

Violence against the person	19.7%
Sexual	0.0%
Burglary	4.3%
Robbery	12.0%
Theft & Handling	23.1%
Fraud & Forgery	6.0%
Drug offences	28.2%
Other offences	6.8%

Prisoners' Offences, Askham Grange, February 1996

NEVER RELY ON A MAN

Born in the 1940s, the daughter of a domineering mother and an easy-going father, I was brought up to 'never rely on a man' - my mother's advice. She must have been one of the first women to penetrate the male dominant industry of woodworking. After the war and after being in a munitions factory she couldn't settle to *women's work* and obtained a job as a joiner. She worked there for as many years as I can remember before retiring. My father was a maintenance engineer and was the original *under the thumb man*.

It was impressed upon me from an early age that education was the most important thing in life. 'You're never too old to learn.' That was another of mother's favourite sayings but one which I think is very true.

Unfortunately, like most teenage children I took very little notice of good advice and although I completed a two year business admin course and got a good educational grounding, I rebelled and became pregnant and married at eighteen. Three years and two children later I was divorced.

Prisoner

MY FIRST CERTIFICATE

I hardly went to school. I used to baby-sit for my mam. There were six of us, I am the second oldest. My older brother left home and went to live with my grandparents when he was eleven years old. Mam left home and I brought the other four up myself. My step-dad stayed and he helped. I used to take them out to the shops and school.

'Look, I've got a certificate.' I remember shouting it out. It was my first certificate - one for swimming. Since then I have collected some more; for bricklaying, typing and now dressmaking. I may be able to use the skills I've learned some time in my life.

Prisoner

THE ETIQUETTE OF ASKING

Personally I avoid asking someone what they are in for, for the obvious reason that it might prejudice me. Of course, length of sentence is a clue. Lifers are in for murder but when you've spotted that you've found out something and understood next to nothing.

What immediately surprises you when you look at the nature of the prisoners' offences in those days is that many of them are no longer regarded as criminal acts. In the 1940s many of the women were imprisoned for activities relating to abortion.

Most avoid that question as though a prison etiquette was operating. Prisoners can tell but mustn't be asked. At the back of my mind is a quotation: 'We are all the people our parents warned us against.'

Brian Lewis

A WORLD UNDER THREAT

The more I became aware of how Askham Grange operates the more I have become convinced that the idea of open prisons for women is sound. I admit to being a trifle naïve - even sentimental. I'm sure that during my visits I talked with a number of hard women, but I was not aware of that. The language has a few different words, the subjects discussed are a bit narrow but in general I would have thought myself to be amongst a very mixed group of women who had little in common with each other, other than their humanity. Some were old, some very, very young - seventeen, some even less - but not one seemed to be a hardened criminal. Reason tells me that some must be, perception suggests that they are not.

I was therefore not a little angry to learn how regulations appropriate to men's prisons, and to a large extent brought about by media coverage of some notorious lapses of sense and of security, including escapes from Parkhurst and Whitemoor, have forced the systems in open prisons to become more and more rigid. That the action of a male prisoner who rapes someone while on a home visit prior to absolute discharge could affect a woman who wants to go home to see her baby is monstrous, yet this is what has happened in the last few months. Liberal and humane regimes have been under such pressure that the whole fabric has been in danger of giving way.

Brian Lewis

One of the most awful parts about the trial was having to show the scars on my neck to the jury. I felt like a piece of meat, going from juror to juror as they craned forward to see.

Sara Thornton,
Love On The Wing, 1996

Meeting the Governor 1968

Stephen McClarence

THE ENTRANCE HALL

A Feeling Of Normality

The feeling of normality unsettles me first. The front door is wide open, there are people coming in and going out. I pass through and everything is normal, everything is unexpected. I may have convinced myself that I came with an open mind but my preconceptions force their way through to assert themselves. The urge to reconcile the normality with the reality becomes overwhelming. I have a strong wish to know why the prisoners are there, I need to be reassured that this is indeed a prison.

My first thought is that the people in uniform working in Reception are prisoners. Then we meet up with Stephanie Slater who looks smart and efficient in uniform and who is in charge of community work. But do all officers wear uniform? We meet a woman in the library. Prisoner or staff? I'm not at all sure. She's not in uniform but she has got a key on a shoelace around her neck. She senses our uncertainty and helps us over it by introducing herself as a prisoner.

Keys are a determinator, I realise after a while. Officers wear theirs in noisy bunches on their belt, those prisoners who are in charge of a key wear it on a shoelace around their neck.

Reini Schühle

Askham Grange 1949

It's a pleasant, rural scene. Three girls on bikes ride through the countryside. A gaggle of geese waddle slowly towards the cool pond. A small group of villagers conduct a leisurely midday conversation. The girl cyclists turn into a wide drive and ride up towards the stately mansion standing in the background.

Many have left school prematurely due to truanting or becoming pregnant, they find that the prison experience gives them new opportunities to acquire a skill. The desire to obtain some practical and useful skill extends beyond the skill itself to boost confidence and increase self-esteem.

Officer

Two of them disappear quickly to change into overalls and get to work. The third puts her head through a door to the front room, which hardly looks like an office, and says: 'I've brought Vera and Rose back!'

It seems almost incredible that the two girls are prisoners and the third is a prison wardress.

Unknown Journalist

Chains And Keys

I have mostly served in prisons for men and it has been a shock to come here almost at the end of my time. I joined the Prison Service in 1969 and have worked in almost every type of gaol - with adults and young offenders. In 1991 whilst with the Prison Inspectorate I was asked to cover at Askham because the governor was ill. Just for a couple of weeks - it has now been almost six years. The needs of women are different from those of men in prison. Most women still try to manage their families, men simply leave the worry of the family to the partner on the outside.

I have known prisons where officers have a key chain which is at least twice as long as it needs to be. Common sense will tell you that for all practical purposes it needs to be the length of your arm but I have seen them twice as long. I have also known officers who slashed the root of their cap peak and re-sewed it so that it almost touched the tip of their nose. They looked threatening. It was all part of a macho thing which is common enough in the army, for at one time many of our officers were ex-servicemen.

I have tried to minimise that, but you will never totally eradicate the need for some to portray a powerful image. I also allow officers to leave off wearing uniform if they need to. A few choose to. Uniform has its

A good personal officer knows her women, will try to help them help themselves. She will perhaps know a woman's family members, will support her in the ups and downs of her sentence, will try to be non-judgmental, will fairly report upon her progress and, if necessary, fight for her when she is in trouble.

conveniences. You can spend a few more minutes in bed each morning if you don't have to think what you will wear. I like to play down the coercive elements while making it crystal clear that this is a prison, albeit a special type of prison.

Harry Crew

HELLO GATE

When the internal phone rings I always say, 'Hello, Gate.' To an outsider I suppose it sounds a bit daft. Anywhere else this would be 'Reception' but in prisons we have our own terms. In the big prisons, ones which look like castles - Armley, Winson Green, Wakefield - where the gates are massive and the paraphernalia associated with entering and exiting are complicated, it is normal enough but here it seems over the top. We don't receive 'direct from court' prisoners here - at least not in an official way - though if they have come up unescorted, transferred from Holloway or one of the other women's prisons, in this office we might be the first people to see them.

It can be a busy area. That is because it is where you greet visitors and hand out keys to staff. Remember also, every prisoner has a key to her bedroom handed to her when she gets here. Keys are a responsibility for everyone.

Linda Marmara

FIT FOR OPEN CONDITIONS

The technical term is that a prisoner who comes here is 'deemed fit for open conditions'. A woman doesn't come to Askham automatically but because she has been assessed. She will usually have come from New

One of the questions usually asked by people who have visited Askham was: 'Don't they want to stay here altogether?' or, 'Don't they commit another crime so they can come back?' The answer is 'No.' They want to be free to live their lives with no more restraint from society than others experience and to enjoy normal freedom.

Officer, 1996

Hall, Low Newton or Risley or one of the top security prisons - Holloway or Durham. She will arrive in a number of ways. She can come with an officer or by herself, unescorted or under escort.

You'd be amazed how much property some of them bring. One African girl arrived at the Mother and Baby Unit with nineteen bags. When she, her baby and two of us, were in the Entrance Room with her belongings, there wasn't much space. Not everyone is like that. Some come with next to nothing. If a woman hasn't got much then we have a store of clothes to help tide her over until relatives bring things through.

You can never tell much about a prisoner from their clothes. Some come looking smarter than the governors, others are really poorly dressed. Since we have gone in for catering for conferences you will see prisoners going about in business suits in this prison.

As many clothes as they can store within their wardrobes are allowed but the exchange of clothing is forbidden because bullying could take place. You could also get difficulties if somebody went off with another's £90 trainers. We have got enough problems without that sort of thing.

On entry a woman will be given a £2 phone card. This is an innovation but a good one. In the old days we would telephone relations to say that a prisoner has arrived. Now she does it herself. That takes pressure off us and gives responsibility to her.

After checking their details and searching them, we allocate them to a personal officer. Everyone here has about eight personal prisoners. It is our job to see they understand rules and to help them out when appropriate.

Then you find them a room. Most have to share - usually two or three to a room, though we try to let lifers be by themselves. About 90% smoke, so there is a problem when you have a non-smoker.

Change is rare in prison - sameness is the law. The same people with the same crime, the same coloured clothes with the same stripe, the same brown-suited guards with the same orders, the same food on the same day, the same disciplinary slips with the same (guilty) verdicts, the same bed in the same cell night after night after night.

Prison Visitor, 1971

Officer

Askham Grange during the First Mini Skirt Age, 1971

I COULD DO THAT

I had been living abroad and so when I saw the advertisement in the Job Centre I thought, 'I could do that,' and applied. Eventually I was called for interview and took the test and passed.

In those days they were recruiting nationally so it wasn't always clear where you would be sent. Now they are recruiting locally. After eleven weeks' training at Channings Wood, and Newbold Revel, the family upped tents and moved here. Now the children have Yorkshire accents and we have the usual small house with a mortgage, so I expect we'll stay.

I love many aspects of the work. I can empathise with the prisoners and all that, but in many ways the job is a trap. That is because, unlike most jobs today, it is a job for life. You get 36 days a year holiday but even that isn't as good as it seems because the most time you can take is two weeks in the summer. There's a non-contributory pension but I often feel that I am waiting for a dead woman's shoes where promotion is concerned. You are trained to be an officer in the prison service. There are not so many transferable skills.

Linda Marmara

IT'S A GOOD PLACE AS FAR AS PRISONS GO

Proving that open prisons like Askham have a good influence on women is a constant problem. It's too easy to see the cost per prisoner and not equate it with the success rate.

Officer, 1997

Here officers treat you with respect and a lot are not used to that. Many of us have come from children's homes - some are very young - and well over half have been abused. Officers can help a lot. They see you've got problems and when times are real painful they are always asking if you are okay. They know I need counselling and they are working to get it for me. My ex has been abusing the kids, disgusting stuff, and sometimes I'm beside myself.

I need this time. I need to have something to occupy me, to turn my mind away from all that has happened. The way they work the system to support you is brilliant. All women's prisons should be like this or some close alternative.

Prisoner

An Office Which Looks Like A Home

The Probation Service is with the prisoner from beginning to end, from the first court appearance to well beyond release. We see her through the initial legal proceedings, bail, entrance into prison and return into outside life which starts when she walks down the drive into the next phase of her life. It is our network of contacts which we hope will sustain her through difficult times and also helps her build a future. We are the bridge between establishments like the courts, police and the prison service and the wider community.

It's not an easy life. Currently there are 126 prisoners at Askham Grange Open Prison but the through-put last year was in excess of 300 prisoners. Some of them are here for a matter of weeks, others are lifers, yet every one who comes here will get similar treatment. Each prisoner has a negotiated supervision plan. It doesn't matter how long someone is here, there has to be a plan.

Unlike the big house built for a Leeds millionaire, our office is housed in a converted semi, it's an office which resembles a real person's home. The village road runs just ten yards away and the gate is open. Inside we have computers and a complete network of high tech gadgetry. The building somehow stands for what we do.

Sarah Wardley

Size of current establishment January 1997:
130 prisoners
including 20 mothers and babies
21 hostellers
2 governors
1 principal officer
5 senior officers
22 officers
plus probation, education and support staff

First Sighting 6 January 1947

The first three months of 1947 will go down in history as the snow and flood period, especially for the West Riding of Yorkshire. I travelled by taxi from my home in Leicestershire to Askham Grange on that bitterly cold morning of January 6th 1947, and as we set out on our journey the blizzard intensified. We sped along as best we could, and arrived at Askham Richard village at noon. The driver had lunch at the local inn and returned home in the full fury of the storm, but did not finish his journey as he, in the blinding snow, met with an accident and was seriously injured.

The prison engineer, Mr Alderson, who had arrived a few days earlier, and a Ministry of Works representative, met me at the door of the Grange. The engineer reported to me that there was no fuel on the premises to feed the fires for central heating. He explained that fuel had been ordered some weeks earlier but had not been delivered. There was no telephone in the house, but I found one in the village, and telephoned the Commissioners about this matter. The fuel was delivered next day.

An officer and a party of men prisoners from Wakefield Prison were dealing with supplies of furniture, household equipment, clothing, stationery, etc that had been delivered during the previous week. All this had been stacked in what was once the drawing room and morning room of the house. Miss Duffy, the steward, arrived during the afternoon. It was her job to check the stock of everything that had been delivered and take it over from the Wakefield officer who had received it from the Ministry of Works. She began almost at once to sort out the books and office equipment necessary to start her work the next day.

In the meantime, I explored the house and grounds, and planned the work for the following day. As there was no accommodation for us in the village, Miss Duffy and I stayed at an inn almost a mile from the Grange. The inn-

Women in prison lack self-confidence and many lack any sense of self worth. They frequently turn to crime - often drug related crime - to sustain a relationship with a male partner and to provide for their children.

HMSO, 1990

keeper had no fuel, and we were obliged to sit in a cold room in our wet clothing until a meal was served. We were shown to our bedrooms afterwards and, to our delight, we found hot water bottles in our beds. At 8.30 am the next day we tramped in the snow to our new jobs.

Mary Size

£14 A WEEK WITH PROSPECTS 1967

The caravan had gas mantles and a foot of snow on the roof, I was being paid £9 a fortnight take home pay for a responsible but dead end job, my parents had moved off to England so this seemed the right time to respond to the advert in the local paper and apply for work in the Prison Service. If the job only measured up to half of what was on offer this was a good job. It was £14 a week, not fortnight, with the prospects of professional training, so in 1966 I applied, travelled down from Scotland and found myself at Askham Grange. It was not what I expected. Instead of being a monster the Chief Officer was a small but very kind woman in her fifties with a liking for lilac, or pink, well tailored suits. She had bleached blonde hair, pink bows on her shoes and swore like a trooper. I had been prepared to be shocked, after all I was an only child, and most things passed over me. The Chief Officer's swearing didn't.

I was really well treated. I was the first ever student to train on the premises prior to going off to the prison officers' school in Wakefield so I was lucky. When my time was up a gang of experienced officers piled into two cars and took me the twenty or so miles to the capital of the West Riding. There they showed me the ropes; they pointed out the cheap but good hairdressers, the restaurants I should go to and the establishments I should not enter.

The secret of success with delinquent girls and women is to deal with them in small numbers. They should be housed in the country within easy reach of a city or town, where it would be possible to obtain land for cultivation and facilities for raising poultry and pigs, as well as flowers, vegetables and fruit. The aim should be to make the institution as self-supporting as possible.

Prison Report, 1947

A week later I found myself with ten girls who had come up from Holloway sitting in a pub called the Blue Lagoon, which had been specifically mentioned by the chief as somewhere I should not frequent. We were watching a procession of drag queens. We giggled so much we were asked to leave. I was a week into my course, the first ever officer to train at Askham and I had been thrown out of my first pub.

Margaret Middlemiss

FIRST PRISONERS 1947

Our first contingent of three prisoners and two officers arrived. The door bell, and indeed all the bells in the house, were out of order. The officers and women walked in through the open door, and wandered about until they found me. I was busy washing crockery in readiness for a meal when they eventually arrived at the kitchen door.

They looked, and I have no doubt felt, bewildered. I took the officers to their rooms, and the women to the dormitory which they were to occupy. Afterwards we managed to provide a meal for them.

Debating our new problem, we began to put our plans for the remainder of the day into action. The women and I went out to collect some sticks in the woodland, and managed to get logs and kindling to make a fire in their dormitory. There was no central heating in their wing of the house. The women cleaned their room thoroughly after the fire was lighted. When the floor was dry, they collected their bedding which had been placed on the radiators in the billiard room the day before to make sure it was not damp.

The officers and I prepared our bedrooms. We all had clean, dry beds and warm rooms to sleep in that night, and Askham Grange was making history. It was established as the first non-security prison for women in the

Women's Open Prisons developed from the Open Borstal system. Open Borstals were for people who could be trusted not to run away. They are cheap to run, with fewer staff and no security to worry about. In the 1940s they were very attractive.

United Kingdom. A revolutionary moment in Prison Reform had been reached.

The Governor of Wakefield Prison had sent food rations for the women. The officers and I pooled the rations we had brought with us, and we managed to provide meals until we could make other arrangements.

One woman was detailed for cookery and table service, and the other two women formed the cleaning party under the supervision of Miss Hoyland, who worked with them. Three weeks later, two more officers and five women arrived. The family had now grown to one principal officer, three officers, eight women, the steward and myself.

The kitchen cooking ranges were unfit for use, and until they had been replaced it would not be possible to take any more women into the house. There was only a small electric cooker in the kitchen of my quarters on which food for fourteen persons had to be cooked.

Mary Size

In Charge

There have been twelve governors in fifty years. Most have been at Askham for at least five years though in one six year period there were three.

Miss Mary Size, 6.1.47 - 30.9.52	Miss J Kelly, 1.10.52 - 3.11.59
Miss M Stocker, 8.11.59 - 30.4.66	Miss P E Wardle, 1.5.66 - 30.11.68
Miss M Morgan, 1.12.68 - 2.4.73	Miss S McCormick, 19.4.73 - 9.9.79
Mr J Whitty, 10.9.79 - 26.7.82	Mrs P Midgeley, 27.7.82 - 11.4.83
Mr J Hunter, 12.4.83 - 20.10.85	Mr R Smith, 21.10.85 - 4.6.89
Mr P Quinn, 6.9.89 - 15.4.91	Mr H Crew, 16.4.91 - present

Many women are horrified by rows or awkward scenes, so they often choose to say nothing rather than risk unpleasantness.

Some women are unassertive in order to make themselves invisible, to avoid drawing attention to themselves, because they lack confidence. Other women are passive simply because they don't accept that they have any rights.

First Sighting 1991

A day at the end of March, clean and bright, but I was apprehensive. To 'baby sit' another governor's prison for a few weeks, and a women's prison at that, did not inspire me. The drive and building looked well kept but I 'signed in' at a horrid hole in the wall - I determined to improve this point of receiving visitors and five years on have achieved that first goal! Initially staff were cautious. I remember one frankly stating, 'You're not here to do your knitting - we expect some involvement from you.'

At that time the Governor's Office was near the Main Entrance and everyone, staff and prisoners, simply barged in - now I have moved upstairs into the area which was once the governor's living quarters and it is a little more peaceful. I think early on it was felt that governors just passed through and were not seriously expected to make an impact, thus it was that there existed an impression that Askham hadn't changed since the 1950s and really, change was highly suspect. The decor was miserable, with not a picture in sight and desks too small with VDUs falling off at the ends. One of the things I did early on was to buy some pictures and try to make people pleased to be at work!

In those days there was a very hierarchical structure. Indeed I remember officers asking me for decisions on minor matters, like making a telephone call, decisions they were well able to act upon themselves. All that has changed.

Harry Crew

We like to have a good relationship with the village and the Governor meets the Parish Council Officials twice a year and tries to attend the occasional Parish Council meeting.

Harry Crew, 1996

Language, Language

When I first got here I thought I was hallucinating; it was so different. The prison I had come from was so filthy that I had used the sponge I had brought in to clean the floor and kept just a flannel for washing. They hadn't heard of bleach there. You were banged up for a lot of the day and at night you slept on a mattress which was like a slice of bread.

Then after a short journey here I was, sitting in the television room with two seventeen year olds who were plotting to abscond. Suddenly the door opened and in came a nun. I looked the other way just in time to see a duck and her little ones walk across the lawn. It was not like I expected.

The other thing which surprised me was the range of women. Some were grandmothers, others seventeen year olds. As you can imagine the younger lot take the mickey out of the older end, and being in between I have to make them see that we are all in this together and we need to support each other. It's a generation thing. When some of us swear - and you need to swear to get rid of your feelings - the older women say things like, 'Language, language.'

Jenny

ALWAYS VICTIMS

Sixty percent of the women in here are victims of male sexual abuse of one form or another. It is important to see this because it forces you into a sort of mind change. It's another area where men and women prisoners differ. We usually think of male prisoners as perpetrators. Of course we know that they can be victims in a very general sense - they have been inadequately educated or their personal esteem is low - but they are usually one step away from being a victim; they create victims.

When you consider women you see that that is not the case, most really are victims of men in a direct sense. A great number come from the same background as the men - they are not well educated, have lived in poor

This is a building with a lot of space but not much room for privacy. The ceilings are high, the public spaces like the panelled hall were built for status. We will never have single bedrooms so we must make areas where women have some privacy.

Harry Crew, 1997

housing, suffer from low personal esteem; put simply, they do not like themselves - so they are victims in that sense; but you have to add to that the fact that they have been abused. Abused in the family, abused in relationships.

Harry Crew

MINUSES DON'T EQUAL PLUSES

Group exercise isn't immediately appropriate for everyone but when it is we often use an exercise which tells us a lot. Together, Probation staff and prisoners draw up a double list with a criminal activity at the top. One half of the page is made up of the pluses which come to you as a result of your crime - money, excitement, holidays, that sort of thing - and in the other half, the minuses. It doesn't take the average prisoner long to see that the advantages of crime are invariably short term whereas the disadvantages are long term; loss of respect, custodial sentences, loss of housing, loss of daily contact with children and a lot more.

Of course, seeing the logic of a situation doesn't mean that you will cease to be a criminal. A lot of personal and social circumstances pull some women back toward crime. Family and friends are not always of help, there needs to be realism. Overload from them and lack of will can destroy the best paced-out probation plan.

Sarah Wardley

I TRUST YOU ABSOLUTELY 1947

At ten o'clock that night I visited the women in their dormitory. They were sitting round a bright, warm fire, sipping cocoa and discussing the new

Adam must have an Eve to blame for his faults.

Italian proverb

A civilised conversation, 1996

condition in which they found themselves. As I entered, one of them said: 'Isn't it lovely, Madam, that we can all sleep in one nice warm room and tomorrow morning we will be able to look out of the windows from our beds without having to climb on chairs to see the sky.'

Another woman placed a chair for me by the fire. I sat down and talked with them for a little while, and then wished them goodnight and closed the door as I left. I had walked some distance along the corridor leading to my bedroom when I heard the patter of feet. Looking round, I saw one of the women who exclaimed excitedly: 'Madam, you have forgotten to lock us in.'

I returned to the dormitory with her and pointed out to the three women that they would not be locked in their rooms at any time, day or night. Our plan was to live together as a family and behave in every way as a decent family should. We would lock all our outer doors at night to make sure that no-one entered the house while we were asleep, and close our bedroom doors when we were ready to retire for the night. 'I trust you absolutely and I feel sure you will never betray that trust,' I told them.

Back came the assurance, 'We will never let you down, Madam, whatever happens.'

Mary Size

There is at least no evidence that fear of imprisonment in itself has any less effect than it may have had in the past on those who have not yet been in prison. As for those who have already served a first sentence, it must again be noted that the great majority do not in fact return to prison. For those who do return, there is no reason to believe that an increasingly repressive regime would have a better effect.

Penal Practice In A Changing Society, 1959

KNOWING WHERE YOU STAND

Askham is an open prison and that makes it different. In a closed prison you know where you stand. You've no responsibilities. There the answer to every question you put to an officer is 'yes' or 'no'. Here it can be those extremes but it is also as likely as not 'maybe' or 'well -'. Of course that's how it is in the world and that's what we have got to put up with when our time is up, but it's not always that easy to have the choice. The reason why some abscond on the first day or so is that they cannot bear the change. The chance to be in charge of yourself drives some close to suicide.

The other choice you don't have here is the choice of privacy. If things are getting on your nerves at Durham or Holloway you can ask to be locked in your cell. Here if you don't want any hassle, you have to put up with things. You can't take to your bed in a safe room unless you are a lifer. You have to share with somebody. Their room is your room. You have no choice about who is allowed to come in. There's no privacy at all.

Sarah

A VICAR IN DRAG 1965

Bank Holidays were really great events. Everyone, including the staff, worked very hard to make sure we enjoyed ourselves. We challenged the staff at sports, challenged them to a Tug of War. We had the Governor - Miss Molly Morgan - on our side. All this took place on the back lawn and the local people came. A buffet was provided and everyone was accepted as part of the village. Miss Morgan always called us her 'girls of the village'. In the evening there was a dance and prizes for the best fancy dress. The Vicar made a grand entrance in drag.

Susan

The Governor was strong upon
The Regulation Act
The Doctor said that Death
Was but a scientific fact
And twice a day the Chaplain
Called and left a little Tract.

Oscar Wilde,
The Ballad of Reading Gaol 1898

A PRISONER'S RECOLLECTION 1949

The interviews with the Governor took place in a small office, with an officer on duty as at Holloway. She saw us first separately and then together.

I knew that the Governor of Askham Grange, the only women's prison without bars in the country, had been Deputy-Governor at Holloway and Governor of Aylesbury Prison and Borstal, and that after retirement from the prison service she had been asked to return to manage what was then an entirely new experiment. I also knew that she had the reputation of being the best of all prison governors. I therefore expected to find somebody looking much older than the figure before whom I stood.

She sat very upright in the chair behind the desk, a middle-aged woman in a well-cut tweed suit. Her greying hair was drawn back in a bun. She wore glasses, and the papers on the desk in front of her were, I imagined, my case papers. She exuded that air of authority natural to those who have held high positions over a long period of time. I sensed that the officer beside her was probably just as much in awe of her as I was. My thirty-six years seemed to slip away from me, and I was about twelve standing in front of the headmistress at my school.

She spoke kindly but firmly about the rules. She told me that there were three exits to the Grange, and there was nothing to stop me walking out of them any day I chose, though she added: 'You would not get far.' For the time being I should be sent to the workroom. After the day's work I would be expected to go to classes in dressmaking or handicrafts, which comprised knitting, leather work and rug making. I was to sleep in the bottom dormitory. She told me that I could have sketching materials sent in, if I was fond of painting, and that I would probably find time for this at weekends.

I said, 'Yes, Madam,' at intervals, but I was impressed by the way she spoke to me. I felt that, even though I was a prisoner, I was perhaps after all still a person. No one said a word about my number, and though I had one it was not mentioned.

Jean Henry

Women tend to put relationships with other people at the top of their priorities. They have career ambitions and achievement goals, of course, but personal relationships often come first. If standing up for themselves and their beliefs threatens relationships with other people, they are strongly motivated to back down.

A KISS FOR NEW YEAR

Everybody tells you the same thing, a women's prison is very different from a men's. I got here immediately after the Christmas holidays and was introduced to the prisoners. That morning it was all a bit formal. The next day was New Year's Day and as I entered the room a prisoner rushed up to me and planted a big kiss on my cheek. 'That,' she said, 'is my New Year's present.' Imagine that happening in HMP Wakefield.

Officer

THE DUCK GIRL 1965

It was not all work and no play, a great many laughs were had by us all. One full-time job was the 'Duck Girl'. We had our own flock of tame ducks. They had to be let out each morning and fed. During the day their eggs had to be collected. Muscovies are known for their habit of covering over the eggs, so you went around with a stick, poking underneath everything. The biggest laugh was getting them back in at night. To make matters worse, the male inmates who worked here during the day would be waiting to return to Thorp Arch Prison, and they would start calling 'clack clack' so the ducks would run everywhere but the right place.

Susan

A LETTER 1992

I must mention what a pleasant surprise both the appearance of and atmosphere within the establishment was, after spending time both in Holloway and Cookham Wood. I felt as though I was being rehabilitated

There's some who cannot take it here. There was one very bright girl - a graduate - who preferred her own space, a single cell, rather than all this communal living.

Officer, 1996

The duck pond, 1971

and helped rather than punished. There seemed to be a completely different atmosphere between inmates and staff - and I, for one, found the majority of staff very helpful, especially the night staff, who were particularly pleasant. The medical staff were also very friendly and reassuring, it was nice to know that they were there to talk to, as well as to take care of the medical aspects. I particularly wanted to mention the Psychologist, who helped me considerably, and without whom I would not have managed my sentence as well as I did.

Emma

ASKHAM GRANGE *1949*

Studying the daily routine, the relationships between prisoners and staff, the work in progress, the women's conduct during their leisure, one almost overlooks the most startling feature of Askham Grange - the complete absence of prison gates or bars or locks, even of a janitor or any security measures to keep the prisoners 'inside'. There seems to be obviously no need for them. Though the prison is truly 'wide open' not a single inmate has as yet attempted to escape. As one of them discussed the imminent date of her release tears came into her eyes: 'I really do not want to leave!' she said. She was one of many who dreaded the circumstances of her own home life, which were responsible for her downfall.

The same woman looked with a genuine expression of affection towards the grey-haired, bespectacled, mild-mannered but quietly self-assured lady whose ideals pervade the unusual atmosphere of Askham Grange. Miss Mary Size, MBE, the Governor (formerly Deputy-Governor of Holloway and Governor of Aylesbury Prison) has now returned from retirement to make a success of the open prison system for women.

Earnings are averaged across the prison population at £6 per week. Some women may earn £8 while others earn £4. In addition prisoners may spend either £10 or £15 per week of their private money subject to the standard of privileges which they have attained.

Earnings of Prisoners 1996

I had a glimpse of the quiet influence which Miss Size exerts. 'Rest assured,' said the woman who had spent one year in Askham Grange, 'that I shall never get into trouble again. I could never let the Madam down!'

There was no doubt that she meant what she said. In fact, only two of the 150 women who have left the open prison have found themselves in court for a second time.

Unknown Journalist

A RATIO OF TWENTY TO ONE, MEN TO WOMEN

In 1997 there are now 2,500 women in prison compared with over 58,000 men and although that figure is rising from the plateau of 1,700 that we had a few years ago due to more violent crime and changed sentencing policy, it's still a relatively small group of people so there is a chance of sensitive attitudes.

Having said that, procedures are getting tighter. In the old days a lot was done on personal recommendation. Remember it is quite likely that an experienced officer like me knows someone in most of the other prisons. The phone will go and a colleague will say, 'I've got this nice girl. Can you take her?' and you do. Occasionally, you have to ring back after a short while and say, 'She wasn't nice at all, I'm sending her back to you,' but that's a rarity.

Officer

The women's prison population is at record levels and is rising. There are 15% more women prisoners than there were a year ago and 50% more than in 1993. Despite the rising population relatively few women are serving sentences for very serious offences.

NACRO, 1996

ARRIVING 1949

We left the train at York. It was just about lunchtime. Now that the journey was over, our spirits had somewhat evaporated. The officer gave up our tickets at the barrier, and we were met outside by another officer in civilian clothes. The Ford brake was driven by a man who, as I learned later, did in addition all kinds of odd jobs in the house and garden. The four of us climbed in the back.

In about twenty minutes we passed through the little village of Askham Richard, with its pond and a couple of shops, and there, facing us, stood our new abode.

There were pillars either side of the entrance to the drive, but the gates themselves had been removed, and there was nothing to tell us that we were entering a prison except a large notice on one side of the entrance headed HM Prisons, and warning visitors and the general public of the penalties that they could incur for assisting prisoners to escape and for smuggling food or cigarettes to the inmates.

There was a short drive bounded on one side by the village church, beyond a wall; and on the other, by a sunken lawn and rose garden. It was a wide, rambling, very ugly Victorian house, and the cold bleak atmosphere of the day did not add to its charm. However, it was a long way from Holloway Prison.

We went in through the front door with its wide porch and were in the hall. It was less ugly inside, with oak panelling and a parquet floor, and a wide staircase to the first floor. I learned later that this was not used by the prisoners; it led to the Governor's wing and the officers' quarters.

Reception was a very different thing to its Holloway equivalent. We were taken into a small office, where our belongings and our cards were checked by the hospital sister who was on duty that day. She told us of various things that we could have sent in at intervals: face-cream, powder, lipstick, bath cubes and shampoos; these would be doled out at intervals when we were due for them; we were to receive nothing in a bottle.

Women are not a minority within our society even if they are a distinct minority in our court rooms.

Helena Kennedy,
Eve Was Framed

The clothes were similar to those worn in Holloway, but were given out as near as possible to fit. You had two of everything, which you marked with your name and kept throughout your prison sentence, unlike Holloway, where you might get anything back from the laundry each week.

After clothes distribution we were sent to get our lunch from a hatch outside the kitchen. The dining-room had about eight long tables, but we were told to sit at a small one until our places were allocated. After lunch we heard that we would see the Governor, and later that day the chaplain. I gathered that all the other women were at work - it was after one-thirty - but as it was our first day we should not be required to join them.

After lunch we were told that we could sit by the fire in the library. It sounded quite fantastic to our ears. The library was a big, bare, uncurtained room with a great many folding chairs and a couple of leather-covered sofas on either side of the fireplace. Bookshelves lined the walls.

A prisoner was doing some cleaning rather half-heartedly and we asked her to tell us all about everything. She wore a blue tie and was called Rose. She came from London - Petticoat Lane, she told us - and her accent was a strange mixture of Cockney and north country. She informed us that the Governor would tell us where we should be sleeping and what work would be allotted to us. The house and garden were run entirely by the prisoners, and you might be put to work in the house, laundry, garden, kitchen or workroom.

It was 'a bit too much like hard work,' Rose said, but on the whole it was better than Manchester, where she had come from, and better than Holloway, too. It seemed that she had known the latter on her first sentence, and she asked tenderly after some of the inmates, none of whom we knew. I named some of the women for whom I had messages and she promised to point them out to me.

The average time spent on remand for untried females has risen from 26 days in 1979 to 44 days in 1989. Many of these women are mothers.

The Governor, said Rose, was all right, 'as long as you work hard,' and the screws 'not at all bad.' It seemed strange to be sitting in a room in a house again and to look out of a window that had no bars.

We asked if it were true that you could earn up to two shillings and sixpence a week? Apparently this was not so. For key jobs only, such as a cutter in the workroom, or for looking after the hens, you could get one shilling and sixpence, but the ordinary rate for the average worker was elevenpence-halfpenny. You could save your money and could then be taken to the cinema in York by one of the officers.

I could not imagine that I would want to go out. The train journey had made me doubly conscious that I was a prisoner. I thought I would take to smoking again, though it would mean only about five cigarettes a week. I did not.

Jean Henry

TAKING YOUR COAT OFF

When I first got to Holloway I wouldn't take my coat off, I was so convinced that someone was going to come through the door and tell me I could go home. I wore it at meals and only took it off last thing at night as I got into bed. I now know that I have to take my coat off and take responsibility for my baby.

Diane

Most of our women come from Newhall near Wakefield, Low Newton near Durham City and Risley near Warrington. These women will have been received direct from court. Other women come from Styal, Cheshire, and Holloway to finish long sentences.

Stephen McClarence

THE BEDROOM

COMPULSORY EXERCISE 1965

Having been selected to come here in 1965 it was stressed to me how privileged I was and in no uncertain manner I was told what the end result would be if I abused this privilege. We came from London by train and our carriage had a reserved sign which stated 'HMP Only'. At York Station the tilly was waiting and in no time we had arrived at the famous Askham Grange. Our first introduction was to be locked in the Quiet Room (now Chief Officer Johnson's office). Lunch was served to us and after the old Holloway's menu it was luxury to say the least. Then it was time to be fitted out with our uniforms. What was the Reception in those days is now the Staff Room. One very important item of our uniform was a black cloak. Those were the days of compulsory exercise. Between one and two o'clock, we all had to go outside and the officers stood at certain points, to make sure we did not creep back in. We tried all manner of tricks not to go out. One was to hide behind the long window curtains. Once outside we had to walk the perimeter of the house so many times. This was done daily including Christmas Day. On a Saturday, if you were a Roman Catholic and wished to attend Mass on Sunday, you had to book for your own clothes to wear. These were kept in the Half-Way House, so on Saturday evening you went up to collect your things and then they were locked in the Quiet Room ready for Mass. Upon your return, you changed straight back into uniform.

Susan

THE MEN ARE PROFESSIONALS

Men let themselves go when they get to prison, women don't. Of course, there is the odd one who doesn't wash as often as she might but she's a

It needs to be recognised that there is in-built discrimination against women prisoners, usually by men but also by women who see women prisoners as bringing discredit on their sex. This discrimination is evident in policies and in colleagues and is not solved by the appointment of a token woman at any level.

HMP - Honesty, Modesty, Purity, 1973

rarity. If a woman is dirty it's because she is ignorant about cleanliness, not because she has let herself go. Most prisoners make an effort and are well turned out. This is because there is a much more varied group of women in prison than men, so they reflect society outside. There are few women professional prisoners in the sense that there are male professionals. I can't imagine a woman saying, 'Just another job governor, just another job. Win some, lose some.' With men crime is an occupation, it rarely is with women. Women often do time to keep or protect a man. Can you imagine a man doing the reverse for a woman? It's almost inconceivable.

Many of the women you will meet in Askham Grange, or in any other women's prison for that matter, are there for one-off incidents. A few might do a bit of fraud but the majority are here for something they do once. That's why the numbers are so small and why every age, qualification, religion - or lack of it - and class, are here. They might reflect the normal balance of society. Male crime by and large is a young man's game.

The frequency with which you hear foul language is also noticeable; you just don't hear the same amount of effing and blinding. There is next to no graffiti and what bit there is is in the bedrooms. The panelling in the Askham Grange corridors wouldn't last the day out in a men's prison.

David Wood

ASHAMED OF CRIME

People ask you, 'What are you in for ?' not because they want to know but because it's something to say when you meet another prisoner. It's like saying, 'What happened in *East Enders*?' or, 'How are you?' It's a way you start a conversation. Some don't want to talk about what they did so they lie. 'I changed the picture on my boyfriend's passport,' says one.

It's strange being a man and working here. You get some really provocative remarks. Sometimes I feel like a bonny seventeen year old walking past a team of building workers.

Officer, 1996

You guess which prisoners did domestics; their sentences make things clear. Not everybody is nosey. Some respect privacy. That's not always the case with officers, some are the *News Of The World*; they tell you what a woman's in for. One girl got a real tough time; not physical or anything you could put your name to, but awful for all that. We learnt the real nature of her crime because an officer, who should have known better, told us.

Prisoner

CRIME SWEEPS PAST

The longer you work in prison the less and less interested you become in the reasons why prisoners are there. The nature of their crimes is known to you especially if, like me, you have once had responsibility for what is called Discipline, the keeping of prisoner records about release and parole, but you tend to get on with the job quietly and I hope efficiently. The drama of crime sweeps past you.

Tucked away as we are in a distant corner of the building we are not in direct contact with prisoners, but for all that we know it is a prison and not a convent boarding school. From Day One when I had my security talk about what you must and must not do - don't leave records about, make sure that computers are not left unattended, don't gossip about your work - I have been on my guard. Perhaps too much so.

There is a family story that when my lad - then at grammar school - was asked at an RAF interview about what his parents did for a living he replied straightforwardly enough about his father's work then continued, 'My mother is a civil servant who is not allowed to discuss her work.' I sounded as if I was MI6 at the very least.

Jackie Brown

This is an old statistic but in 1979 30% of untried and 47% of convicted unsentenced women aged 21 and over remanded into custody were subsequently given a non-custodial sentence or freed at court, compared with 23% and 32% respectively for men. Things won't have changed much.

WHEN JUDGES GET OUT OF BED

The way the judge feels when he gets up in the morning determines the sort of sentence you get - that and if you are a man or a woman.

My husband was in the dock with me; he got nine months, I got 16 months for the same crime. It was totally unexpected; my solicitor had told me that although it was DHSS fraud I wouldn't get banged up; it was my first offence, I had children of school age, was responsible for my mother - she was partially sighted and 72 years old. Also my dad had recently died. The kids were at school. 'I'll be back by dinner,' I said as I left. I had fiddled £25,000.

The following week the same judge had sentenced a woman for taking the DHSS for £37,000. 'You're lucky,' he said, 'last week I gave a woman 16 months for less than what you have done.' She got a suspended sentence.

Prisoner

A LITTLE BOY AT HOME

I didn't expect to be put away. I had one nine year old boy and my daughter Phoebe was eight months old so I was distraught when the judge gave a two and a half year sentence. I was being ripped away from my family and although I knew that my husband and my parents were supportive I cried and cried. It was a first offence, the type of crime which wouldn't be repeated. I had spent fourteen months waiting for the trial - a sentence in itself - admitted guilt, done all the sort of things that should get you a lenient sentence and had the book thrown at me.

Like anyone going to prison for the first time I had no idea what it would be like. My views were coloured by television - *Cell Block H* stuff - and I

Imprisonment is an expensive sentence both in terms of the cost of maintaining the prison system and the indirect costs incurred by families deprived of financial, emotional or social support. It is estimated that the average cost of custody per week in 1988-89 for female offenders was £399. By contrast, the 1987-88 average costs per offender per week for community service, probation and supervision orders were all under £20.

Home Office Report, 1992

Outside the Mother and Baby Unit, 1976

expected to have a lot of hassle. Fortunately someone told me that I could have Phoebe with me if I applied and the authorities were sympathetic. After I got the forms things moved very quickly; I reached New Hall on the Tuesday and my little girl was with me on the Saturday.

Many people - outside people - must find it hard to see why Phoebe should be in prison with me but I am convinced that this is the best solution. Of course there are problems but these relate more to my boy; he misses his mom and I truly, truly miss him. Phoebe has a good life, plenty of fresh air, the crèche, long walks in the countryside, professional attention when I am doing classes to give me the new skills I'll need outside. It's doubtful if I will get similar work in my old profession. I go home once every month, soon to be fortnightly when I get to the hostel, she gets a lot of attention and does not seem to have suffered at all by being in here with me.

Wendy

DRUGS

Many men take drugs because they want to experience something new, a lot of women take them to blot out memories. That might be sexual abuse as children, rape as adults by family members, providing alibis for lovers, storing their drugs, becoming a prostitute to support a man. They take to crime because of men. There are prisoners in here who have heard their men say, 'If you want money for that little bastard get on your back and make it.' Some men turn to petty crime to support their families, but not a lot.

Their demand for love for this reason is great. A woman is dependable, a man isn't in the same way. A man will swear love but often cancel a visit at the last moment. He'll phone and say, 'You don't mind if I don't come,

In Askham about a third of the prisoners have been involved in theft, a third involved in violence and a third are involved with drugs. 60% have suffered abuse - usually sexual abuse, 50% have children under 16 years (25% are under five years) and 82% retain no home outside. Yet most won't reoffend. That's why we will take any age or offence on a sale or return basis.

Margaret Middlemiss

England is playing Scotland,' or, 'I had a hard night's drinking yesterday,' - probably he's found a blonde down the road - or, 'I would have to get up too early.' A woman would never do that. She'll have the kids up at the crack of dawn and be queuing outside.

'If he put petrol soaked rags round her neck and lit them why does she bother?' I asked. 'She says that she loves him,' came the reply.

David Wood

Love Is Blind

I had seen him before in various pubs but never had the chance to speak to him. He really stood out from the crowd, he was tall, well groomed, nicely dressed. His stance and his stride were so different from any other I'd seen before. I couldn't take my eyes off him. The DJ played *Crazy* by Let Loose and he started to dance with his mates. Eventually I got chatting to him and he invited me back for coffee. I couldn't resist. I'd never known myself be so attracted to someone. At the flat we chatted for a while, then the inevitable happened. He told me his name was Darren, he was aged 26 and lived in Yarm in Cleveland.

I saw him quite a lot after that although it was never classed as a relationship because neither of us wanted any commitment, but we were together most of the time. He'd be at my house, or I'd be out somewhere with him.

As time went on I found out his real name was Stewart and it was soon to be his 21st birthday. I also found out he lived not far from me, in Stockton. We celebrated his birthday in our local night-club and had a brilliant time. I was devastated when I found out his age, but I liked him so much I brushed it to one side. I am 36.

In an age of data collection and computers the number of children whose mothers are sent into custody each year is unknown.

NACRO Report, 1991

After a few months I found out he was involved in drugs: We were in our local night-club when he took ill, I could see him holding his chest. I asked him if he was okay and he said he was. I kept watching him, then suddenly he looked like he was really in pain, so I suggested we leave.

He asked me to take him to hospital. On the way there, he lost all feeling in his left arm and leg. As I pulled up outside the hospital he was slumped against the window. I thought he was dead.

The nurses got him into a treatment room and when he was stable they let me in. He looked terrible, although he was awake, he wanted me to take him home, but the nurses wouldn't allow it, they said he'd stopped breathing five times already. I stayed there until 4.45am when I was told he'd be alright. So I left and tried to get some sleep. I later found out he'd taken three Ecstasy tablets, a steroid injection and alcohol.

Soon everything started to go wrong. I was lending him my rent money, my car, he was never off my phone. The truth dawned: I was, and am, in real bother. I had a £300 phone bill and a £900 rent bill, neither of which I could pay. Luckily I have good parents, they bought me a little car to go out and do my mobile hairdressing.

On 9th February 1996 the bomb shell dropped. I was sentenced to 18 months imprisonment. Stu was in court, he just stood there and looked at me. I couldn't speak, I was devastated. My father had just had a heart attack and my parents knew nothing about all this. I was taken to Low Newton Remand Centre straight away and eventually here.

I've never seen or heard from Stu while I've been in prison. I think about him a lot; I wish he'd get in touch. I know he's really messed my life up, but I can't forget him. I'd love to see him once more. There's one thing I've learned from all this: it's true what people say, love is blind.

Jackie

A higher proportion of women than men sentenced to immediate imprisonment have no previous convictions.

Home Office Report, 1996

GOVERNED BY THE BELL 1949

After the interview, I was given a pen and ink and the single sheet of paper used for the prisoner's reception letter. Visits were once a month, as in Holloway, but owing to the length of the journey for most people one could save up two visits and have an hour every two months.

I did not look forward to the dormitory, but I had also had to get used to this sort of arrangement in the hospital at Holloway. Judy told me that she was in the same dormitory, and soon we were sent there to make up our beds. It was a room on the ground floor leading out of the hall. There were seven beds.

At four-thirty a bell rang, and prisoners went tearing down the passage to get tea at the hatch. You were handed your plate, with the familiar thick slice of bread, dab of margarine, and sometimes jam or lettuce, and on Sundays perhaps a scone or piece of cake. One woman from each table took weekly turns with the teapots and filled up all the cups at her own table. We four newcomers sat again at a little table for our tea, as we had not yet been allotted places. We were all in a rather nervous, giggly state.

Classes took place in the workroom, library and the ballroom. I thought it sounded very peculiar talking about the ballroom in prison. It was a very large oak-panelled room, with a stage at one end, which was used for concerts.

We felt very bewildered on our first evening. Supper, which consisted of cocoa and bread and jam, or bread and dripping, was at eight, and though I went to bed directly afterwards it felt incredibly late. I was too tired that night to take much notice of the other women in the dormitory, and when an officer came round to turn out the lights at ten o'clock I said good night to Judy and very soon fell asleep.

50% of the women at Askham Grange have no previous convictions at all. For 50% the experience is their first-ever time in custody.

because some men are very supportive when their partner is at Askham Grange, men have let the prisoners down. No wonder they turn to other women for friendship.

There's too much concentration in the general public's mind on the physical aspects of female friendships in prison and not enough on its quieter, less intense manifestations. Yes, of course there is the occasional predatory lesbian; of course some manifestations of loving go beyond what is tolerable when others are around in a place that doesn't afford much privacy, but generally these are contained.

Harry Crew

QUIET MOMENTS *1949*

I realised as I lay awake in the darkness that for the first time since I had been in prison I was no longer afraid. All the time at Holloway I had been frightened. Afraid of the key turning in the lock of my cell door, afraid of the grim faces of my gaolers. Even in the hospital I had felt that trembling nervousness that recoiled from the screams in the night and the naked misery in the eyes of many of my companions; fear of giving way to that suppressed hysteria which is part of every woman's make-up; fear of madness and melancholia, and of the terrible dreams that are part of the long night; fear of the gradual deterioration of the decent human instincts that separate human beings from the animal world; and a haunting fear of the future, in a life that saps initiative and encourages lethargy. In some ways I had enjoyed advantages in life which made prison existence harder for me than for many, but in other ways I was better equipped to cope with it. Was I exaggerating, I wondered? I did not think so.

Jean Henry

Reformation is a journey, not a destination. No one can state definitely that a certain percentage of women who had served prison sentences are permanently reformed. We can only assume from our experience of them that, as they had given of their best and shown the proper attitude towards the rights of others while in our care, they will continue to do so in their new sphere of activity.

Mary Size, 1951

Stephen McClarence

The Chapel was once the billiard room

QUIET MOMENTS

At the moment the library's a haven for those on the intellectual side who want to read a paper or a book. It's a place for a nice select group of people. You put the lamps on at night and sit down and read - it's really cosy, like a family house. Those that come in here don't go in the TV room. You get the older ladies.

I make a display of six books a week, ones which I've read and reviewed myself, which I call *Charley's Weekly Selection*. There are a lot of women who come in and they want a straightforward review of the book. They want to know if the language is easy. I pick a pretty mixed batch, and things that have been on telly. The classics aren't totally popular.

Charley

MAKING THE BEST OF MY TIME

Ordinary people go to prison, always remember that. As a visitor I am always impressed by the normality of the place. Some women are bitter, some, I'm pretty sure, are twisted but there are also courageous women; women who have spirit.

It's the humanity I love. Women who have obviously wrapped men around their little fingers making a brave attempt at twisting me. Women who have been submissive and shy continuing to be shy and withdrawn. Young women who could be a daughter, women I really enjoy talking to, women who are vivacious and attractive, women who are a bit of a laugh. Brash, vulgar women; intelligent women; they are all there in Askham Grange.

Sometimes statements get made which leave me, as the saying is, gobsmacked. After one woman had gone on and on about the injustice of

Censorship is virtually unknown. Prisoners have access to all books in York libraries.

her sentence, a woman across the table very quietly, not arguing if she herself was guilty or otherwise stated, 'I'm going to make the best of my time in here.' She seemed so very dignified.

Prison Visitor

I Don't Cry Easily

I didn't cry when I was picked up, I didn't cry during remand or the trial, I didn't even cry during my stay at Holloway or Styal Prison or here at first. I did not cry until they came and told me that my mother had died and then I started to cry. I cried first for my mom, then for my lost opportunities; I cried because I was in prison, I cried and cried. All the way to the funeral I cried and I cried all the way back to Askham Grange.

I was inconsolable. That night my mates lay upon my bed and held me as I cried and cried and cried.

Prisoner

A Crying Woman 1957

Behind the woman's tears was this story. News had just reached the prison that one of her children had died in hospital. Her husband had phoned through demanding to speak to his wife. This the Governor had refused to allow, telling him that it was against the rules, but that she would deliver any message he cared to send his wife.

Against the rules! Surely in the circumstances this particular rule could have been relaxed? It seemed inexcusably heartless that at such a moment a husband might not be allowed to comfort his wife. But, as it happened, the inexcusable thing was that I should so have misjudged the reason for

'It is well known,' Judge Sutcliffe reminded a jury in 1976, 'that women in particular, and small boys, are liable to be untruthful and invent stories.'

Helena Kennedy,
Eve Was Framed

The Governor's Stairs, 1950

this official attitude, which was subsequently explained to me. Far from wanting to comfort his wife, the husband, drunkenly, had declared that he wished *she* had died, and wanted to tell her so. In the past, apparently, he had often assaulted her, and she had had just about as much of him as she could stand, poor woman. All that could be done to comfort her was done by the prison staff. A priest she asked to see was immediately sent for, and arrangements were made for her to attend the funeral, a long train journey away. This required careful planning; in her distressed condition she needed someone with her on the journey, nor could she be left without protection from her husband, whose behaviour when he saw her was not to be trusted. The sympathy and concern felt for this unhappy woman was so evident that for a while I could not put her out of my mind. And in my mind, too, was the thought of how strange it seemed that the cheerful atmosphere of the prison should be disturbed by what was happening *outside*.

Sewell Stokes

The Government Inspectorate of Probation found in its 1991 Report that women, ironically, sometimes received harsher sentences than men because they were mothers. They may be deemed unsuitable for community service because they have young children, but then the courts, unable or unwilling to come up with an alternative punishment, send them to jail.

Helena Kennedy,
Eve Was Framed

LONELY SAD WOMEN 1980

You have to be in prison to see how the other half live. I've known women who've never had anything approaching a family Christmas; gifts, that sort of thing. Someone out of the family was always in prison.

It's no wonder some do strange things. One woman just disappeared. We thought that she had absconded but she had somehow found a way to hide in the space between the floor boards. She lived for six days on bread and butter mints and then let us know she was there. She got extra time for that. They said she was guilty of 'secreting herself'.

Ann Thistleton

THE ARSONIST 1994

She had a toy boy of fifty, herself was in her seventies, had spent her life in and out of prisons, so when she got here after having been sentenced for arson, we were all a bit worried. I asked her straight out: 'You are not going to burn this place down, are you?'

'No,' she said, 'I only burn down old folks homes. I like young people.'

Officer

SHE JUST WORKS IN THE GROUNDS 1950

Askham Grange has been in and out of my life since I was a girl. My dad took me there just after it was opened and I used to sit in his car, EKL 945, and wait for him as he went inside collecting insurance from one of the officers. Once I saw a woman in the grounds with great staring eyes, a giantess of a woman carrying an axe. You can imagine how I felt. I pulled myself low under the seats and waited for her to pass by. I would have been about eight at the time, and very scared. I asked Dad about her when he returned. 'Oh,' he said, 'she's alright. She just works in the grounds.'

Ann Thistleton

MOTHERING

Unlike at a lot of other prisons you have to learn the ropes yourself. It's not like at New Hall or Durham where you have a book which lets you know everything so that when you are first banged up you can read the rules. Here you learn the rules gradually, like you do in life. People help you understand, not books.

A number of those suspected of committing criminal offences are mentally disordered. The government's policy is that wherever possible such persons should receive care and treatment from the health and social services.

Home Office Report, 1990

The central stairs, 1996

CLOSE THE DOOR?

If you are in a normal prison then you know where you stand and you can go into a cell and close the door. Not here. Some people prefer closed prisons for just that reason.

Of course there are support systems. Older women, women in their forties and fifties, help younger ones; mother them if you want.

Prisoner

BULLYING

Bullying goes on in a number of ways. Mostly it's emotional bullying, rarely physical. Quick-witted women gang up on less able ones and make them uncomfortable, freeze them out. Sometimes you don't know what you've done to deserve the treatment. One woman for instance took a lot of aggro because she snored in her sleep. Another smelt and wasn't too keen on washing. Bullying on the other hand might be nothing other than somebody wanting to be evil.

There was this girl who had just one picture of her man. She put it on the side of a locker and opened it so that when she was in bed she could turn her head and look into his eyes. She decided to move in with somebody else and did so without telling the others. She took all her belongings, cleared out but accidentally left the picture - funny really, it would have been the first thing I would have taken, he looked lovely. When she went back it was gone. I told her to assert herself; to go and ask them for it. She wouldn't, she was too scared. 'Shall I go in and get it for you?' I asked.

'No,' she said, 'it's easier to write and ask for another.'

She'll have to learn. It wasn't as if they were going to trash her room.

Prisoner

The balance of training has altered over the years. We have always trained officers in First Aid, now we also have sessions on Addressing Offending Behaviour, Drug Counselling, Managing Aggression, Hostage Negotiation and Time Management.

Officer, 1996

SITTING ON THE STAIRS 1984-96

I'm 43 and the other night I was sitting on the stairs counselling a sixteen year old about alcohol. 'Look here,' I said, 'if you don't sort this lot out you are going to be like me in a few years, sitting on the stairs counselling a sixteen year old.'

I'm a bit different to the others, I have been in and out of prison since I went to my first Borstal. I've been to Askham several times, most are first timers and do not come back. I don't know if I'm going to break the habit but the one thing I have noticed in myself is that for the first time I seem to be telling the truth about myself to myself and to others. I am admitting that I've got problems, real problems. Askham encourages you to do that. That's to do with it being fair. Here, if you admit to something - you know the sort of thing, you're feeling depressed and think that you might be tempted to abscond - they try to understand. I've been in prisons where the answer was to bang you up. In most prisons I would not put my hand up for anything. Here I can speak honestly, in other prisons I tell a pack of lies. In other places they don't seem to know what's going off. One has installed a fruit machine where there are kids who are addicted to fruit machines, another spent a lot of money on mountain bikes not thinking that they were ideal for anyone thinking of escaping.

The honesty and the openness are one of the reasons that Askham hasn't got a serious drugs problem. Of course there are drugs but it's nothing like the problem I've seen elsewhere. I once ran off from one prison because I was trying to stop and it had more drugs than anywhere I had ever been. Here you can't afford to take drugs. If you are caught you get the Gipsy's warning and then you are back to closed conditions. Even if you are like me - the judge called me a one woman crime wave - you don't want that. Yet drugs aren't the worst there is; drugs, especially pot, are

The offence patterns of males and females are strikingly different, showing that women in general commit less serious offences than men. However, there is now a trend amongst women to physical violence. I blame it on the clothes, I call it the Doc Marten Syndrome.

Officer, 1997

understandable. Bullying gets you shipped out even faster. And quite right. I wouldn't think twice about having a bully shipped out. I might be a persistent offender; someone with no hopes, no home and a lot of major problems but I'm better than any bully.

I also like the idea of having a personal officer though sometimes it can be funny. I went to mine recently and you know how women go on, after a time she was telling me her problems. In the end I had to say, 'Mrs - no names mentioned - you've got every bit as much trouble as I have.'

We laughed at that.

Gillian

IS THE PARTY OVER?

Somebody advised me when I got the job: 'Never lie to an inmate.' Therefore, as soon as I have got a woman sitting down at a drugs counselling session I put down some ground rules. I say, 'I know that you are going to lie but will you keep it to the minimum? If you've got a heroin problem then talk about it. If you lie too often, just as you can't trust me I can't trust you; the party is over. I'm not prepared to waste my time.' One-to-one counselling - four people one hour once a week - is very time consuming.

I also know that I have two responsibilities, one to the prisoner who is trying to come off drugs, the other to security. If I think she is about to say something that might implicate other inmates I warn her not to go too far; I'm not interested. Mind, because Askham is so small there is not a lot that one of us doesn't know.

I'm not into drug counselling so that I can improve my record as an officer but because I want to help a prisoner kick a damaging habit. Apart from all

The expectation of what the Prison Service can achieve in reducing drug misuse must be realistic. Just as in the community, it would be unreasonable to expect prisons to eliminate drug misuse. Persons should however aim to reduce as far as possible the amount of drug misuse.

Home Office Report On The Misuse Of Drugs, 1996

else, women on drugs have a lack of self respect. I put a lot of emphasis on this aspect of my work since many of the women in here are prisoners precisely because of drug-related crime. I argue strongly that you can have anger counselling, offending behaviour and assertiveness training, but get them off drugs and you are tackling what is obviously a major problem and often the root cause of their crime.

Sometimes I sit as a counsellor and sometimes as an officer. I'd argue that if a woman says to me that usually she has done four heroin on average last month but has only done two this month then that is an improvement and to be worked on. Nobody gains if I slap some punishment on at this point. Also, you have got to see that this would break trust and affect all on the support team.

Most women want to be honest in what is clearly an extremely difficult situation.

Carol Sturzaker

AS COMMON AS SMOKING

You got to face it, many of us come from places where doing drugs is just as common as smoking, and where there's not much else to do. Most women blend in with what's around them and drift into it but once you got it it's not all that easy to kick the habit. A lot of women are in here for drug-related stuff. If they were given degrees for their knowledge there'd be plenty of caps and gowns walking round in here.

Drugs come in, they're bound to. You just can't watch everybody all the time and anyway, even the most rigorous search policy has got some loop holes.

Prisoner

Some misusers take drugs for the first time inside prison but the number leaving prison who misuse drugs is lower than the number entering.

Home Office Report, 1996

JUST THROW AWAY THE KEY

I was sitting next to this woman the other day at a meeting and she said to me, 'If I had my way I would lock them up and throw away the key.'

'I'd be sure then,' I said, 'that you don't knock someone down going home and kill them, or that when you skid you don't get arrested smelling of your one glass of sherry.'

I thought of a young nurse, who was traumatised for years after she had got up on automatic, following a night of steady drinking six days after the break-up of a relationship, and had killed a woman on a zebra crossing. Or Karen, who went over the speed limit, like you and I probably have today. The difference was she skidded and killed her best friend who was in the passenger seat. I doubt if she got up that morning and said, 'I think I'll kill my best friend today.' She was going off to university that year, she came to Askham Grange instead.

Emma was also a nurse. Her boyfriend had gone off leaving her in the final stages of pregnancy with £7,000 debts. A middle class girl, she decided to pay off the debts, got a day time job and, having bought in a baby minder, got a night job as well. Unfortunately, she was still on the dole. She got done for DHSS fraud.

Ordinary people go to prison.

Carol Burke

No punishment inflicted by law is for the sake of harm but to make the sufferer better, or to make him less bad than he would have been without it.

Plato, 429-347 BC

Stephen McClarence

THE NURSERY

TARAXACUM OFFICINALE

My dad, Patrick O'Reagan, worked for Harold Wilson at Chequers and as a lad I used to take his Labrador Paddy for a walk, but for all that prestige and with the pick of the gardeners at his disposal, he never had a workforce who was better than this group of women who work with me. They are wonderful to be with and a great laugh; they're bright and want to learn, especially now that they are doing NVQs.

Last week one asked, 'After we have finished that job do you want us to tackle the *Taraxacum Officinale*?' Well, as you can guess, I didn't know what they were on about. When I got my qualifications you were expected to trot out a few Latin names for shrubs, trees and garden plants but mostly you used common names. This, I guessed, might be a weed but unlike them I didn't spend night after night learning about horticulture. 'Yes, you'd better,' I said.

They laughed. They knew that in this sphere at least they knew more than I did. That night I checked the name out so that next morning I could say with confidence, 'Tackle the *Taraxacum Officinale*.'

And they did. They chopped down the dandelions.

It's a pleasure to come to work.

Garry O'Reagan

A CHAPEL IN THE BILLIARD ROOM

The conversations which take place in the prison chapel are not necessarily spiritual in the old-fashioned sense. We provide quietness and the space for a woman prisoner to understand herself, we are not into peddling religion and indeed women from other faiths are welcome here. Obviously prayer

Three other prisons have Mother and Baby Units, Holloway, Styal and New Hall. Mothers can keep their babies with them for eighteen months but then they have to be sent out of the prison; some go to foster homes, others go to relatives or to their father.

Officer, 1997

is important but we do not push doctrine at people. That seems inappropriate. Women come to us in great distress and we offer a place where they can be quiet.

Sometimes, six at a time, they go for forty-eight hour retreats with a religious order called the Sisterhood of the Holy Paraclete at Sleights, near Whitby. Taken seriously that can be very fulfilling. On a retreat all is given to total quietness, reflection and thought.

The Chapel is close to the Mother and Baby Unit.

Roger Clegg

GOD IN A BILLIARD ROOM

In the alcove behind the chapel altar there is a frieze of fat cherubs, and above this: AMO PAX. Close by there is a painting of Christ preventing the stoning of the woman taken in adultery. I'm not sure what the chapel was originally, a billiard room I think. I know it was used as a morgue during the army occupancy. It is a small oasis. One prisoner said to me, 'The chapel's my other sanctuary. I've learned to find my own places, to get away from situations other people might be creating.'

Frances Brett

600 MILES AND WE NEVER LEFT THE BALLROOM

For twenty-four hours from Friday afternoon until Saturday afternoon, the prison became obsessed by rowing. Teams composed of staff and prisoners sponsored by other staff, prisoners and relations, attempted to row 600 miles on rowing machines in aid of the Marie Curie Cancer Fund.

It's noticeable that the babies in the unit are well in advance of babies of a similar age. This is because they are constantly with other children and learn from them. They also have the undivided attention of a number of adults, the most important their mother.

Officer, 1997

Breaking our rowing record for charity, 1996

At the beginning some outside teams also participated: Emperors Gym York, St John's College and Yearsley Bridge Adult Learning Centre, but after about 11pm it was an Askham-only effort. The complete prison population participated in some way.

Prisoners and staff came and went during the night; Tom Naughton, a Deputy Governor, visited at midnight, Kathryn Dodds, our Principal Officer, visited with her husband during the evening. I came in at about 2.30am, bringing fruit. Matt Dodd, our Board of Visitors Chairman, visited at 6am.

Not everyone was absolutely clear about the reason. One of our young ladies was heard to say, 'Marie Curie is a woman who is dying of cancer and this sponsored row is to raise a bit of money to help her.' She was in the minority and everyone understood that effort was being put in to help others. In the end they raised £644 - a terrific effort which, I am sure, gained a lot by a sense of individual achievement, and also by improved relationships - it was very much a team effort.

Askham Grange has raised thousands of pounds for charity in recent years, mainly at the two Open Days - a Summer Fair and a Christmas Fair, but also through events organised by the PE Department.

Margaret Middlemiss

A GREAT WHITE HORSE

Although sport and physical training has been a sort of Cinderella subject - there hadn't been a full time PE officer for several years when I got here - things are picking up. The absence of a spacious gym is still a problem but I have now got a hockey and football team going on the grass which used to be the vegetable patch. Rounders is very popular.

I got into fashion drugs - Ecstasy, cannabis - it was just for fun really. Then I got into a rut, started dealing and couldn't get out. 'I did the crime, I'm doing the time,' but I also know that I need to be in an open prison and get some education at the back of me. There are so many barriers to employment if you don't have education.

Prisoner

Probably the most beneficial aspect of the work are the outings. Sometimes these are low level events such as the countryside walks, at other times they are major trials like the John O'Groats to Lands End cycle ride for charity. By most people's standards they are small scale, 874 miles at a cost of £500 plus a lot of organising time, but you need to see how the prisoners develop when personally encouraged.

The other Saturday I took four on an expedition to Sutton Bank. It was a reasonable day but one of the lasses insisted on keeping her anorak on as we toiled up the side of the Great White Horse. She said she might catch cold. There was a lot of 'How's the family' talk with Marjorie who is 48, and an equal amount of grumbling from Karen who is 20 but when we got to the top the view was spectacular. You could see the clouds themselves and their shadow moving between you and the foothills of the Pennines. I had seen it before and been moved but they were seeing and experiencing something new, and not the mean streets of Leeds and Bradford, places where they came from and eventually would return to.

Sue Blackburn

GOVERNORS IN KAFTANS 1970

The women would be sitting in front of the fire in the hall at the bottom of what used to be called The Governor's Stair when the Governor would appear from out of her flat - governors lived in rooms which are Admin now - and walk down towards them dressed in a beautiful kaftan.

'Good evening ladies,' was her greeting. They might have been effing and blinding seconds before but they'd shoot to attention with a 'Good evening Miss.' That governor had been a teacher at Roedean Public School.

Ann Thistleton

Although we have had women who take degrees and 'A' levels we now concentrate our efforts on National Vocational Qualifications (NVQs) and have a high success rate. Last year we achieved a 100% pass rate with Dress-making students.

Education Officer

TWO SCHOOLGIRLS

I knew it was her as soon as I walked into the room. We had been in the same class at school twenty years ago but I recognised her immediately. She was scrubbing the floor and so didn't see me. I said nothing but turned and went straight off to see the Governor as you are bound to if you recognise someone from your past life. She weighed up the case and decided that there was no need to have her transferred on. It was the right decision. She's never given me a moment's trouble; in fact I spent this morning teaching her to swim.

After we finished school she went one way, I went another. Vivien found herself a man, got a house, did reasonably well, was respectable until her man got a habit - crack - and she started to thieve to feed it. She lost everything. When she got here her personal esteem was rock bottom. Most of the women here are like that.

I was luckier. A teacher took an interest in me, saw I was a natural sports player; county standard at senior squash, and a good team player. This, and the army, gave me a start and I eventually arrived here in 1989. We came from the same part of the city, lived in similar housing and had good families. Two girls. I was the lucky one.

Sue Blackburn

WELL DONE

Women are different to men when it comes to sport. Give a group of men a football and they'll rush around all day, give them a gym and they'll pump iron. Women aren't like that at all, they have to be coaxed. You can't improve standards by shouting in their faces, 'Come on, come on, you can do better than that,' you have to give them incentives. For many that means loss of weight.

Women should be consulted about the kind of activities provided. Thought should be given to the inclusion of games of ethnic origin, such as Kabbadi. If there is a swimming pool then it is important that they have access to attractive costumes. Women can be sensitive about their appearance in swimwear.

Home Office,
Regimes for Women, 1997

Meeting the Governor

Sometimes this job brings real moments of insight. There was this girl and although she was pleasant enough you could tell from her behaviour that she had had a rough time. Remember, 80% of the women in here have been beaten up by some man or other so their sense of self-esteem is very low. They also come from groups where there is little praise. Perhaps that's why a lot don't make eye contact when you first meet them.

I had set up the gym and given everyone a schedule. As I went along the line I said to this one woman, 'Well done Eve, that's really good.'

'What did you say Miss?'

'I said I think you are doing very well, well done.'

All she said was, 'Thanks Miss,' yet she said it in such a way that I knew that nobody had ever said that to her ever before.

Sue Blackburn

The children of imprisoned parents have been described as the hidden victims of the justice system. They may be taken into care following a parent's imprisonment, a circumstance which seems more likely to follow the imprisonment of the mother than the father, and suffer the trauma, stigmatisation and behavioural disturbances that can be the result of such a course.

Home Office Report, 1990

WE DO MORE THAN VISIT

Board of Visitors is a term which in many ways has outgrown its usefulness but having seen the alternatives we at Askham have decided to retain the nineteenth century title. It came about because when prisons were local they had to be inspected by *visiting* magistrates who would look at their administration and hear grievances. We still have the right to come into Askham unannounced.

Of course the term *Board of Visitors* is confusing. There are, for instance, Prison Visitors - people who are attached to the chaplaincy who help prisoners but have no authority beyond their individual interests. We are close, I suppose, to a Board of Charitable Trustees or a set of School Governors. We are volunteers who cannot receive pay, but we are not personally liable, thank goodness, for the finances of the prison. You can see how the problem of the title arises. Words like inspector, trustee, monitor, governor or independent have to be avoided because they are either inaccurate or describe something different which is already recognised in the prison service. When our national organisation came up with four alternatives we found them either too long-winded or inaccurate.

We are best defined by what we do and who we are. In a nutshell, we are members of the general public - people from a variety of backgrounds - who are interested in the welfare of the entire prison community; both staff and prisoners. We are independent of staff and management and are directly appointed by the Home Secretary. Our work varies. Prisoners get a leaflet about our work and how to contact us, and many use the service. If prisoners feel that they are misinformed or they want help we are on hand.

The other month a prisoner wanted guidance about visits to see her partner in another prison. She thought she had a right, others thought it was a privilege. We sorted it out using books in the prison library. By herself she might have got bogged down in the technical language, together we found that she had a mandatory right; she could insist on making the visit.

Matt Dodd

Not Quite A Barrow Boy

Askham Grange has an ethos all of its own. It's partly the fine building and grounds which cannot fail to touch the women living here and partly the character of the present Governor. He's a very visible and approachable presence around the building. He will chat to anybody (slackening though rarely breaking his step!) and he regularly - and quite uncharacteristically for governors - joins the women for lunch in the dining room, where you

Thankfully, women and men in grey suits have not figured greatly in the development of the Askham ethos.

What staff have to share in a prison like this is an interest in people and in particular, the women prisoners' needs. Governors and officers don't have to come from one social strata. Take the governors:

One was a law graduate, one a self-confessed reformed alcoholic, one a public school mistress, one a social worker and another, a finger print clerk. One was a governor in her early thirties.

will find him engaging in a kind of barrow boy banter with them.

Typical of the philosophy is the Forum, an evening meeting between prisoners and the Governor, supported by one of his senior officers. To an outsider, the spectacle of the prisoners airing their various grievances to this seasoned pair, who address what genuine problems they can but more often roll with the punches and throw a few back, is wonderfully illustrative of the skills each side develops to survive institutional life. Sessions are goodnatured. And useful. There is a mutual respect. The women learn there is a great deal they can do to improve life for themselves. And the Governor himself has to live within a set of rules.

Rhona McMeekin

THE CASE OF THE MISSING TOILET PAPER

The Forum is a good place to let off steam but because we have new prisoners who pass through on a short term basis many of the problems which get brought before it are old chestnuts. Insufficient toilet paper is one. I know that it gets nicked to clean off make-up and for a whole variety of purposes other than for what it was intended. It's the trivial that gets to some of my colleagues and occasionally to me - but it's important to them. The organisation of the phoning out system, essentially an initiative of the Forum, proves the worth of this gathering and I am all for it but at the end of a long day nit-picking can be tiring.

At the last one the whinging got to me and I answered back with such directness that one of the women got up and left the room. This produced such a furore that one of the women said, 'Mr Crew, you shouldn't have lost your temper like that. You're the Governor and should set an example.' She was right!

Harry Crew

In 1995 the cost per prisoner-place in Askham was £18,903; this is at a time when the national average wage is £18,000. The cost of running the Mother and Baby Unit accounts for this figure. Take this out of the equation and our cost per place would be reduced to £16,331.

Annual Report, 1996

Prison Officer's Uniform, 1973

LIFE BEGINS AT FORTY

Although I had done a lot of jobs in my time, including being a policewoman when I was young, when I got made redundant on my fortieth birthday I decided to join the prison service. I've been here almost as long as the Governor. I know that because when I tried to get accommodation in the village I discovered that he had already taken the only room.

I love the work, mostly for its variety and because it is useful. It can also be a laugh. Although I only did a short time working in Armley I was there long enough to know that there are differences between a women's prison and a men's. I don't doubt that the men have family problems but generally their concerns are with themselves. 'I', 'me' are favourite words in there. You are often aware of their selfishness. 'I've got a problem,' is how a lot of conversations start. In a men's prison there is a pecking order. In here, especially in the Mother and Baby Unit, things are different. Women focus on their families and children rather than on themselves.

The unit is supportive and, because there are a lot of children around, the babies mature quickly. That is fascinating. If a woman has nothing she gets kitted out. The children develop quickly with one exception, learning to talk. With so many grown-ups about watching their every need they don't bother to talk. Get them outside and they come on in leaps and bounds.

Carol Wood

The Governor does not have parental responsibility for a child in a Mother and Baby Unit. The aim of the units is to recognise that responsibility for the care of the child lies with the mother. Remember, babies are not prisoners.

Kathryn Dodds

GLAD WHEN THINGS GO RIGHT

The problem arises when discipline is involved because normally things are quite relaxed. The normal rules of a prison have to be observed;

antisocial behaviour, shouting and swearing have to be slapped down. In the final analysis, if things are not satisfactory, although you might start by asking for improvement, in the end you have to tell prisoners where they stand. At our best we are like an old-fashioned extended family, there are rules of good behaviour which are there to help everybody. Prisoners can have debt counselling but they have to make the decision whether to get into debt when they are on the outside. We can talk about self-reliance but *you* have to take the steps to be reliant *yourself*. I can be glad for them when things go right and be sorry when they don't, but I'm human, I cannot resolve their problems.

Carol Wood

AARON'S BIRTH

It wasn't my first - I've Tia who is two - so I knew that I was going into slow labour on the Saturday night but concealed it from my room mates until the Sunday. They got me into York on the Sunday and Aaron was born soon after, weighing in at 6lbs 10oz. Naturally I was scared. My family was a hundred miles away, but you have to get on with it. My mom and my partner were there the next day. Everything went well from there on.

The Mother and Baby Unit is really good. I've my own room and plenty of time to look after Aaron. He's coming along nicely. Last weekend we went home on a compassionate for the first time. The family fetched me. It was wonderful and although I knew that I would have to return to prison it was worth every minute. I brought back some jeans and left my maternity clothes in Cumbria.

Kelly

When a man is absent, the family home can be kept going by his wife if she is provided with sufficient money and general support. But when it is the woman who is absent, the husband is often unable to cope and unless there are relations who can take on the housekeeping and care of the children, the home may have to be broken up and the children scattered, either into the care of the local authority or to different relatives.

HMSO, 1977

The Dining Hall, 1949

DAY CARE

We are a bit different from other women's prisons. Here a prisoner can work and use a day care system similar to one that exists outside prisons for women lucky enough to access it. The prisoner sleeps in a room with her baby but just before the start of the working day she takes the baby to the crèche and picks it up during the major breaks and in the evening. She does not have great amounts of unstructured time with her baby.

The fact that the Mother and Baby Unit is in another part of the prison from the crèche helps. Even if it is only a couple of hundred yards across the grass, it is a slightly different world and the staff are not the same. Throughout any week day there is a lot of toing and froing, strapping in and out of push chairs, changing clothes to cope with the weather, just as there would be if you were making for your mother's house down the road.

Officer

THE END OF SEPTEMBER

My father and my husband named her with one of our traditional names; she is Laila. She was born in prison and has been with me all the time at Askham.

Eighteen months seemed a long way off when Laila was a baby but now she is growing I know that it is time for her to move on from here, though it will be a wrench to see her go. She's very forward, climbing everywhere; and there are few toddlers. Most are babes in arms. She needs to be out of here, I know that, but I also know how I am going to feel. Once the date was eighteen months away, now I have it clear in my mind. It is scarcely a month away.

Yasmin

Our childhood conditioning teaches us women that as the nurturing, caring sex our needs come second, and we feel selfish and greedy when we think of ourselves and make demands or say 'no' to a request. By the time we grow up, it is second nature to put our own needs second when dealing with men, or indeed with anyone in authority.

Stephen McClarence

THE CLASSROOM

NEGATIVE AND POSITIVE TIME

In life, as well as in prison, time can be divided into two: *negative time* and *positive time.* When a woman gets here after being in a closed prison she has a lot of adjustments to make. Usually she has come from a closed prison where she has been locked in a cell - terrible to you and me but to some, preferable to a dormitory - and in there she has been confronted with masses of negative time. Cell life can be especially corrosive. If she doesn't watch it she can be dominated by the feeling that she is worthless and that others are there to look after her. She risks losing any sense of personal worth or responsibility.

In the induction period here she has to make adjustments and these include key decisions which will affect her use of *positive time.* Again, this is not an easy thing to do because since sentence, or in many cases since remand, the right to chart her own destiny has been taken from her. When she gets to Askham she has three days of induction and this is where she must make crucial decisions about the use of *positive time.* All of the staff who have oversight of the allocation of positive time have a part to play, though our agendas are slightly different.

Carol Burke

VARIOUS PROGRAMMES

Each section of the prison can present programmes but it is the prisoner who must come to a conclusion about what she *needs* both inside and outside when she has served her sentence. She must look at the options and then enter into a contract with one department or another. In the Education Section we offer a variety of options including hairdressing training, garment work, business skills and food management. These sit alongside

Sometimes, on an evening when I am in the dorm, I get out my Business Administration work and get ready to knuckle down and stress my brain for some work to wordprocess the next day. This is serious work that I enjoy doing as it passes the time away fast and ends my boredom.

Prisoner

classes in English and numeracy. National Vocational Qualifications (NVQs); degree study and other Higher Education options can be pursued. I see no hierarchy in this list. Degrees are sometimes more relevant than numeracy classes, sometimes vice versa. The criterion is *need*.

So what is my job? In this process I am the practical person who negotiates routes through a social and educational tangle; if anything, I am an educational strategist who knows what is on offer and frequently a route which will move a woman on towards a destination. Sometimes the route may be long term, sometimes more short term, though even short term ones can have long term implications. Working on a project like the quilt project - the final product hangs outside my room - is a case in point.

Carol Burke

TALK OF EDUCATION

I am here for thirteen months. That gives me a chance to do something new, but I think the Education Unit is good for people with short sentences too - they can start something off in here and carry on when they get out. I had an ordinary education, but I have eight 'O' levels altogether. That's normal education at home. In our house, expectations are high, you have only made it when you get a university degree. When I finished my exams I had had enough of school. I left but I regretted it later. I think most people want to go back to school but can't because of children and looking after the home. It's not good to have been in prison. Even without the opportunities of the Education Unit I would have been better off on the outside. But if you have the facilities, it's best to make use of them to your advantage. I am just trying to make things better for myself when I get out.

Prisoner

I've got to keep a three bedroomed house and my four year old daughter. I will expect her to study, do 'O' levels and to go onto college. I want that normality. I'll make things change for her, for in our family the women expect to be housewives.

Prisoner

EDUCATION BOTH AS WORK AND FUN

Our wall hanging was funded by our Regional Arts Board, Yorkshire and Humberside Arts, who paid for a professional textile worker to work alongside prisoners. Out of this came a number of exercises which went into the portfolio which a long term prisoner submitted to a college when she wanted to become a fashion designer. She is now a five days a week student in York studying on a degree course. What dominates the thinking inside this unit is recognition that the education provided is not a gift but *an entitlement.*

As you would expect, a lot of the women, especially the younger women, want to go to college. Their motives vary but many want the status which goes with the student life, it is a psychological and social need as much as an educational one. They want to say to their friends and family, 'Look, when I was given a chance this is what I was capable of.' I am not being negative when I say that the majority cannot match their expectation to their ability and nothing I can do can help them. There are expectations but the majority were not nurtured in childhood and in early schooling to achieve much in terms of formal education. So now I have to show them what is realistic, no more no less, and it is in that spirit that we make progress.

Some things are only my responsibility in an oblique way. Everyone here is responsible for inmate development as far as anger or stress control is concerned but ultimately the responsibility for looking at these aspects of the prisoner development rests with professionals in another department. Of course I take part in case conferences but I am primarily concerned with formal educational routes.

Carol Burke

Trish, my teacher, says that these paintings I'm doing now are big enough for me to have an exhibition. I would like that, although even now a lot of my pictures are on display in various rooms up and down the prison.

Prisoner

I really enjoyed maths and I'm good with figures. I would love to go to college and do finance or accounting full time but I wouldn't be able to afford it. I have sent off for the prospectus for evening classes and I will probably keep myself and my daughter by doing clerical and reception jobs and not go back to shoplifting.

Prisoner

I MIGHT HAVE WON OSCARS

I just went to an ordinary comprehensive school. I only took English and Drama because I liked those subjects best. Domestic Science was okay as well. Most of the time I nicked off school but I never nicked off when it was Drama. I wanted to do Drama when I left school. My mother always said that I was a good actress. I'd have won all the Oscars. I should have done Drama after I left school. I don't know why I didn't.

There wasn't a drama school near us, maybe that was it. I went on a YTS scheme instead and that really buggered me up, it nearly did my head in. On the YTS scheme they gave me a job in an old folks' home and I nearly killed a 103 year old woman. She couldn't do anything - nothing at all - for herself. They asked me to feed her and I was trying to shove these carrots in her mouth. She nearly choked, she was turning blue and everything. No one told me that her food had to be liquidised first. I left after that. It was awful. I went into barmaiding next. I've done all sorts of things. I enjoyed working in a pub but we got some real nutters in. I used to give tips. My dad was a bookie and the customers asked if I had any tips. The first time I just told them any name. It came in at 6 to 1. They all gave me a part of their winnings so I carried on. It was great.

I like doing the course here at Askham. It's not like school. I got expelled from school at least four times for nicking off. At least I can't get expelled from here.

Prisoner

CHAMPIONS OF COMMON SENSE

I am not keen on the term *basic education*. I was once the little working class girl, who when asked by the slightly elitist English teacher, stood up and truthfully announced that me and my dad took the *Sunday Mirror*. That was a mistake. I have since learned that I was expected to say we read the *Observer* or the *Times*. She tried to make me see that as people we, me and my dad, were pretty basic and low brow. If you have ever had that sort of experience then *basic* conjures up a class of dunder heads. I avoid using it.

I like to think of myself as a champion of common sense. It might be normal for most trainee chefs on catering courses in traditional colleges to wander around with a full kit of carving knives but not for a prisoner from Askham Grange. It is me who has to cope with the tabloids if I ever risked it. I need neat footwork for I know I have to negotiate a pathway which is as dignified as I can make it and which does not offend anyone's susceptibilities.

The Education Department is the bridge between *prison* and *release* so we always have to remember what awaits many of the prisoners when on the day of their release they cross that bridge. Some of my goals must seem somewhat negative. They are not, they are realistic. I must ensure that women do not come out of here with unrealistic expectations. Many, when they walk out of the gates, are going out to homelessness and poverty such as we on the outside would find it hard to imagine. Not only do some have to overcome guilt and shame, but they are moving into instability from an environment which, for all its faults, is stable. This is the common lot for most women prisoners. The majority of men who leave prison go back to women who have waited for them and, as far as they are able, have nurtured the family. This is not the case for the majority of our women. Not only are they going back to environments where they are known to be ex-prisoners but they will have few financial resources to sustain them. In many cases the men will have moved on.

Carol Burke

Sometimes my brain is ticking over, drafting out a story. Fiction is the best type of story, I think, for really making the time fly. Your imagination runs wild and you sort of imagine you are there; your brain creates all different kinds of images of characters and scenes.

Prisoner

NOT A GIRLS' SCHOOL, A PRISON

Just before Christmas I had my car stolen with all my presents in the boot. It was found somewhere at the back of Killingbeck Police Station. I was full of negative thoughts, I can tell you, when I got there and these did not go away. The car was smashed up, a total write-off. Now, however, what remains with me is not the anger of losing it at such a difficult time but the image of three small boys; five year olds, seven year olds, stalking round it looking for another bit to rip off and destroy. I go home to a house with home comforts. Many of our women come from that area of Leeds where my wreck of a car was located.

I like the work, my colleagues are a pleasure to work with and I enjoy being with the prisoners. The surroundings are beautiful and our classrooms well designed. So much so that sometimes as I come through the gates on a spring morning - the sun on the village pond, the trees leading to the gate in blossom - having left the mayhem of home, the kids arguing, the washing up in the sink, I think, 'I would do anything for three weeks in here, no responsibilities, everything done for you.'

That's when I pull myself up and need to be reminded of the negatives. Askham Grange, for all its excellent qualities, is still a prison.

Carol Burke

THE HANDICRAFT OFFICER 1948

Miss Daisy Powers, a Matron in a boys' Borstal institution, volunteered to serve at Askham Grange, and was transferred about six weeks after the opening of the prison in the rank of Principal Officer. Her experience in teaching handicrafts to Borstal boys proved valuable. Shortly after her appointment to the staff, she and Miss Dobson both offered their services

In the 1940s and 1950s agriculture used to soak up a lot of prisoners - Borstal boys used to go onto the land or into prison camps. Since then farming has become a highly technical industry and there are next to no farm labourers, therefore fewer outlets on release for employment in agriculture.

Officer

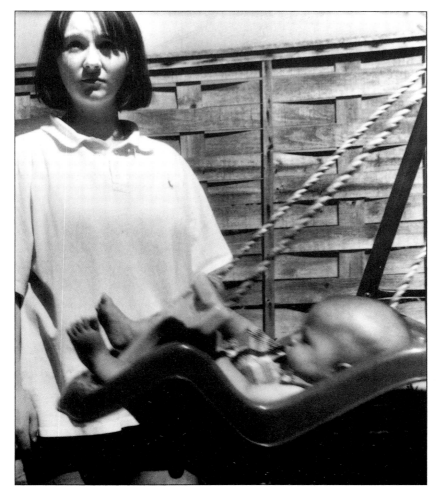

Stephen McClarence

The Crèche at the end of the gardens, 1996

as voluntary teachers. Miss Dobson who was a qualified dressmaker, taught needlework and dress-making, and Miss Powers gave tuition in various crafts such as rug-making, canework, knitting and crocheting. I brought some oddments of leather and tools from home and taught leatherwork. Materials for handicrafts were difficult to obtain and those that were not rationed were very expensive. Parachutes were obtainable. We bought several of these, in silk, rayon and cotton. We unpicked them and made ladies' and children's garments out of the best pieces. We dyed the rest in various colours and used them for rug-making. The silk parachute cords we made into bathroom mats and lace curtains. Training in cookery and housewifery started at the beginning of March 1947. One of the officers, who had trained in these subjects at a technical school before the war and who had worked as a cook in one of the women's services during the war, undertook this work. A syllabus was prepared for each subject and arrangements were made with the Local Education Authorities to hold examinations after a twelve weeks' course. The first examinations were held the following June, the results of which surpassed our expectations. The highest award was 85 per cent and the lowest 60 per cent. There were no failures.

Mary Size

LIKE A GIRLS' SCHOOL 1949

Walk through the grounds of Askham Grange - ten acres of woodland, gardens, potato fields - and mingle with the inmates who, apart from their age, might be a collection of schoolgirls. Some are taking a course in first aid. Others are digging potatoes or tending the roses. In one of the pleasant, spacious rooms of the house a handicraft class is in progress. Many hands are busy in the kitchen, preparing the evening meal and at the same time

I don't like relying on anyone else and so I try out anything and, wherever possible, get an NVQ. Once I went on a building course on which there where ten men and me. That's when I built a wall and learned mortaring.

Prisoner

acquiring the subtler art of cookery and housewifery. Another group is just learning how to polish floors to perfection - and the women are proud of their success. Dress and toy making is being taught, embroidery, leather work, laundering, shorthand typing.

Unknown Journalist

NOT LIKE A GIRLS' SCHOOL

I don't see it like a girls' public school. The women here in 1996 are too various for that. There are grandmas and bits of kids, women, who when hearing someone say 'bloody' say, 'Wash your mouth out,' and others who swear like furnace men. There's no uniform and that for me is very significant. A girls' school would be all starched blouses and regulation skirts, here it's comfortable clothes. The complete ethos is not about conforming but about learning to stand on your own feet and putting together the personality resources which will let you do that. Of course there is structure. Probation planning is a priority, as are the community and education plans, and that sort of organisation is similar to that in a well managed girls' public school. These women don't pass examinations, they get on with life. The major resemblance to a girls' school comes when you start talking fees: it's very expensive to have a woman imprisoned here but if 85% of women moving out do not reoffend in their first year - always a vulnerable period - then that has to be cost effective in every way as far as society is concerned.

The building - oak panels and shields with bits and bobs of Latin - might make it a bit like Cheltenham Ladies College but buildings never tell you much. Forget the public school bit, if it's like anything it's like a well managed comprehensive school for grown-ups.

Brian Lewis

Boredom is the problem. I hate weekends. Jobs - whatever jobs - at least give you something to do.

Prisoner

This Education department is open 50 weeks of the year. Evening classes are available four nights of the week. There is catering, a hairdressing course and one that concentrates on business studies in the morning and dress-making in the afternoon. Between 30 and 40 women are normally engaged on day time education, with a small number following courses at external colleges.

Officer

PRISONERS IN BUSINESS SUITS

'Your conference facilities were described to me as the best in North Yorkshire. I can confirm this statement.'

This letter about the prison as a conference centre makes me proud. As part of their education the responsibility of organising something like a day conference for a group of health visitors or probation officers is one of the most exciting things that many of the prisoners have ever done. I lead from the back; all the main decisions - letters of acceptance, sending maps, organising menus, setting up the room, ordering stationery and reception - are made by them. Recently I was away and rather than cancel, one of the prisoners took over the management of the whole operation. What a morale booster. Many of our younger end have never been able to find meaningful employment. This is the most interesting work they will ever do and it's real. Of course we do systematic business skills courses, NVQs, that sort of thing, but this is extra; it's not role play, it's for real, and the responsibilities are significant. Nothing ever goes missing and occasionally our women have as much as £200 in their hands which they pass on to us.

On conference days they meet the world as workers. It's not unusual for a delegate to ask, 'What's it like working in a prison?' They don't recognise that the woman in the smart business suit at reception, or the well dressed woman waiting on table, is a prisoner.

Alexis Hanford

PINOCCHIO'S NOSE

Derek Lewis came on one of those inspections and in my best manner I explained that everything was made in the kitchen, nothing bought in. At that, in all innocence, he went across to a woman making parcels with filo pastry, the one thing that we do buy in. She had heard what I said and didn't want to let me down: When he asked her if she had made it she said she had. Then he asked how. I could feel myself going redder and redder but she kept her end up and described how to do it. Wonderful. Mind, I'm like that: I jump in, worry myself silly and then everything turns out right.

A couple of months ago they were opening the York Probation Service Building in Lowther Street and somebody asked us to do the catering. Of course we had done some complicated jobs inside the prison - conferences, even a wedding - but this was different. In the first place I couldn't take just anyone, the prisoners had to be ones who were allowed out. In the end I managed six - two heavily pregnant and Bev, the life and soul of any party. There were some hiccups. I couldn't get a driver because of sickness and we ended up causing a traffic jam as we scraped the van along a wall. In the end we got through and presented a polished menu - sandwiches, bits on sticks, dips and crudités, vol au vents - which was so good that the Archbishop of York and the High Sheriff came into the kitchen to thank us.

Carol Carter

MAKING MEN'S PANTS 1946

The workroom was a pleasant, light room - obviously once the drawing-room when Askham had been a private house. There were five electric-power sewing machines facing the windows, and behind these two treadle machines. The rest of the room was occupied by long trestle tables, with a specially large one for cutting out at one end. At the far end a small space had been partitioned off to form an office. Judy, Mrs Mackay and I sat down at the nearest table which was reserved for learners. Mrs Butler had been sent to work in the garden. The head of the workroom, Miss Batten, was not an officer but a sewing instructress. Prisoners in all prison

Man shapes buildings and buildings shape man.

W S Churchill

Cookery class, 1949

workrooms in this country are engaged in making mail-bags and shirts, pants, handkerchiefs, ties and other garments for men prisoners. All these articles have to be made exactly to pattern and standard measurements. You had to do a certain quota a week to earn your pay - for hand-sewers elevenpence-halfpenny a week. The quota was very high. My fingers were stiff and sore after the first few days. In addition to this work I was doing dressmaking from six until eight in the evening, so I hardly ever left the workroom. However, I soon got used to it, and the time went much faster than on any other kind of job. Before long I was promoted to a treadle machine. I had never worked one before, and at first I was very slow and despaired of ever getting out my quota. But I was determined to master it, and for the first week I was as stiff in the knees and thighs from the unaccustomed exercise as if I had been riding or cycling every day. Later, when one of the women on an electric machine was due to go, I was told that I could move up in her place. It terrified me at first. I felt I was driving a car over which I had no control. It was not long before I put the needle through my fingernail, but in the opinion of the other women no one became a fully fledged machinist until they had done this, so I felt that I had earned my wings. Eventually I was turning out seven shirts a day, or two hundred and fifty ties, or the full quota of whatever we happened to be working on at the moment. Every Friday I bought five Players or seven Woodbines, all of which I had smoked by lunchtime on Saturday. I gave my dog-ends to Judy.

Jean Henry

ONE OF THEM A LIFER

The job of making clothes and teaching about fashion brings its own rewards. Once, in a search for new materials for a fashion show we were

I'd like to thank you for giving me a chance on the lifers' garden. It allowed me to contribute something towards the 'system' that has done so much for me. It was nice to know that someone had a little faith in me and trusted me enough to allow me to work outside normal working hours.

Sally

organising, three women and I went off in my car to Colne in Lancashire to look for new materials. We broke down on a cold winter's evening somewhere on the Lancashire/Yorkshire border. I remember thinking as we pushed the car, 'How did I get to a point in my life when me and three prisoners - one of them a lifer - are pushing a clapped-out car towards a roundabout?'

We do all sorts of things: we study costume at the Lotherton Hall Museum, take relevant NVQs and organise the wardrobe for the prestigious York Mystery Plays. Everything gets done with enthusiasm; that's because I believe that unless you enthuse yourself I don't see how you can make prisoners enthusiastic. It needs to be a shared effort. Fortunately I have done a range of things in my life - run businesses and shops starting from next to nothing - which have forced me to learn a lot of skills; so I can say with confidence there's other ways of making a living before you have to go thieving.

Jenny Farley

DAUGHTER - A JAILBIRD

Well, me dad says, 'This place wain't learn you nowt!' And it won't. They should have left me at New Hall Prison if they wanted to punish me. I weren't afraid of New Hall but then I've never been afraid of anyone or anything in my whole life. If I came in crying as a kid my dad kicked me back out and said to defend myself. It's the way I've been brought up, to take what life throws at you and put up a fight. As for stealing, everyone on our estate nicks, it's a way of life. I think my mum's ashamed of me though. Daughter - a jailbird.

Prisoner

There is no point in locking up, throwing away the key and then one day turning women loose who are unprepared for life outside prison.

Progression into the world is essential. Women have to have time to prepare for housing, employment and changed family circumstances. A transition stage is essential.

Tutor

A REAL PROBLEM

We sometimes get very bright women who, because of the nature of their crime, cannot return to their old profession. You know the sort of thing, nurses who cannot nurse because they have been certified drug users.

A subject like word processing and business studies offers them an intellectual challenge and the chance to enter another world.

Officer

SOMETHING I MADE THEM

For me, being in the Education Unit is to do with keeping the links with my family. I have got seven kids at home, the older ones look after the little ones. I am making pump bags for my kids now. At least when I get home I can show them something that I made for them. I don't see this as a chance to get educated. I would never be able to use an education with seven kids. I have a twelve week old baby. When I get her I can have her with me all day in the Education Unit. I can put her pram right here in the classroom.

Prisoner

NOT MUCH HOPE

When I get out I would like to go to college and do sociology or something but I haven't a hope in hell with the kids. There's no point in trying to do it in here. You need to concentrate and I can't think about anything but them at home. Being on the Unit might help some people get a job but it won't help me. I don't have a job, unless you count looking after the kids.

Prisoner

A humane visiting system is an integral aspect of the Prison Services objectives of maintaining links with the community and looking after prisoners with humanity. This is essential to maintaining good order in a prison.

Home Office Report, 1996

House maintenance party, 1949

Doing What I Wouldn't Do On The Outside

The Education Unit is good. It's good for a job when you get out and you can find out things that you can do. In here there is plenty of time to do things, things I couldn't do outside because of the kids. That's the main problem with education on the outside unlike here. There are no nurseries for them to go to while you're in the classroom.

Prisoner

A Wonderful House, But Not Home

Now there are two places where I live: my real home, and my room here. I've made it mine, but it isn't a place I can relax. I spend a full working day in the Education Department, then time with my baby, then back to the room and I'm still not alone. There's me and the baby. And anyone can come in. Even when I go back to my family for visits I still feel tied to this place. It is always pulling me back. When I'm here I'm thinking of home, when I'm home I can't help thinking about here. I have no feeling for it - I don't want to have any feeling for it, I don't want it to win. It's a wonderful house, but it isn't home.

Prisoner

I don't know more than three women who have been through the Askham Hostel and have gone back into prison.

Officer

THE WORLD

FACING THE WORLD 1959

The first real offender that I knew was a boy who used to come home with me when I had first started work. My mother would make him a square meal and we would talk. He had really seen life from the rotten end, had been in institutions all his life, first Dr Barnardo's, later Borstal. One night he called in looking dreadful. 'What's wrong with you,' I said, 'you look as if you've got toothache?'

'I have,' he said. 'I tried to take it out with some pliers but the tooth broke so I couldn't get it out and now it's even more painful than it was before.' He then went on to explain that he had wandered around to a number of dentists but had been too frightened to approach 'women in white coats' for help. I took him round to my dentist. Ten minutes after he had gone through the door, he was out grinning all over his face, bloody but minus the offending root.

I often think about that story. He wasn't thick, he was just naïve and because of his life history, he had no sense of independence. He had lived all of his early life in institutions so when he wanted a dentist he had asked someone who was in authority and one had quickly been provided. He didn't have to explain, he didn't have to organise himself. He was institutionalised, and - as it will - the institution provided.

In prison you constantly have to watch that prisoners do not fall into the trap of knowing that the authorities will provide. Life outside isn't like that and they have to be protected. As I see it, Askham Grange's outreach community runs directly counter to institutionalised life. Women who work on one of our schemes emerge from the placements with a greater feeling of self worth.

Harry Crew

Regimes, as understood within the male prison estate, are not transferable to the female estate. Women prisoners made it clear that while regime activities are inportant... what is happening on the outside is much more important than what is happening on the inside.

NACRO, 1996

THE COMMUNITY PROGRAMME

We set up the Time Shop in December 1992 as part of the Prison Charity Shops Trust. It has been a wonderful success and I wouldn't be surprised to see other prisons develop similar schemes in other towns. Of course York is ideal for such an initiative.

I am a bit prejudiced when it comes to talking about York. I've lived in the city all my adult life, brought up my three girls here and this is the place I love. I came to work in the prison when the children went off to school and I have never really wanted to move from Askham. I suppose that is what makes me especially useful when it comes to community development. I know my patch.

I don't think that I could cope in a closed prison; I like to have the prisoners round me, working towards an achievable goal. I know that there has to be sentence management if we are to get anywhere and make a serious attempt at sensitive rehabilitation. I am also experienced enough to see that it can't be too soft edged; it has to be realistic. That's where my common sense comes in. Ever since I got my pip I have seen my role to be working to get any community initiative off the ground. I have specialised in that and when you look at the programme you can see that we have achieved quite a lot. The prisoners all bring to the experience what they have learnt before their sentence and you have to match their background to what is on offer. There is one woman who doesn't like men, any men. I say to her, 'If I had had your experience I wouldn't like them either, but the world is half filled with men and you need to know how to deal with them because I'll tell you this, they won't go away.' She's as strong as an ox and loves open-air work so you give her a chance to work in the country. You don't agree with her but you put her in a situation where she can develop in isolation at her own pace. There's nothing that makes her more

'I'd like to go into journalism.'
'We all have our dreams.'
'Well, you did ask.'

content than reclaiming an overgrown pathway. We planted out 1,000 bulbs this year for the superintendent. He's a lovely bloke. She is not dismissive of him.

Another woman likes working with animals so she is working at the RSPCA in their animal shelter five days a week. Weekend work is involved there but we manage to get her to work by using the van if the bus service isn't convenient and it never is on a Sunday. That's the trouble with being in a rural community, public transport is not much of an option.

It has been the making of her, that's because she gets a lot of dignity from feeding and grooming in the kennels and cattery. It's wonderful to see her giving tender loving care and attention to animals which have been ill-treated and abandoned. She brings her work home with her to such an extent that I have found her a six foot shed in the grounds where she can keep her birds and a rabbit. She's a real animal lover and much taken up with ferrets.

Stephanie Slater

AFTER JADE LEFT

When Jade was born I was in constant dread of the day they would take her away from me. Askham is such a small prison that everybody knows of my worries. The rules are strict and clear. A prisoner can keep her baby with her until it is eighteen months old and then it has to move out of the prison.

I'm not saying that what happened helped me but at least someone kept their eye on the situation.

Mrs Slater could see that I would be devastated by the experience so on the day Jade left she arranged for me to start work on a community scheme. I

Yes, it's a nice place but it's a prison. Always remember that, for underlying that statement are a lot of tears.

won't say that it eased the pain, nothing could do that, but at least it took me to somewhere new and away from the Mother and Baby Unit. I went to work in the Probation Offices in York.

The job in itself is simple enough. I do a bit of cleaning - hoovering mostly - and supply everybody with cups of tea and coffee but it takes me out of myself to see that the world is going on out there. It is pretty routine really. It's up at 7.00am and down for a bit of breakfast - toast and cornflakes, nothing fattening - before we pile into the van and move off to York. It is never crowded. This morning, for instance, there was the two Rachels, Nora, Chris, me and a couple of prisoners who needed to be dropped off at the railway station because they were going on home visits. Two were going to the Time Shop, one to the cemetery and the other somewhere else. It is alright and it has got me over a hurdle but I still live for home visits and the chance to see my small daughter. She's lovely.

Prisoner

SQUEAKY CLEAN

Of course there are hiccups. The Community Programme works, but naturally nothing experimental runs without some risk. I suppose that as a prisoner the main problem is that you have to be squeaky clean to work on these projects. As you can imagine prisoners get up to all sorts in prison - and, let's face it, so would you and I if we were prisoners - but they can't afford to on community work. As an officer you understand the temptations but you have to be strict. There are phones on hand and people will try to communicate with prisoners by writing to the work address but the sensible ones know that they must not step out of line. Any abuse of privilege falls not only on them and on me but on the project as a whole. There is no way I will put this project in jeopardy because of some

After 18 months babies leave the Prison. In 1995 one went to an aunt, another to a foster home. Their mothers were still serving sentences at Askham Grange.

prisoner's unthinking action. I know that anything that smacks of rehabilitation will always have its critics and it is very easy to cut off the oxygen on a project like this. Anyone with an understanding of the issues involved will see that the public awareness is shaped by the information surrounding men's prisons - escapes, abuses - but the powers that be are not discriminating; they don't see the distinction between women and men. If the press and the politicians want to convince everybody that prisoners are dangerous we bear the brunt for the men.

You can't be everywhere. One couple on a Community Programme spent all their allowance on going and getting sunbed treatment. I understood why they did it but I could not allow them to get away with such action. If I had done so in this climate of public opinion I can see the headlines in the popular press now, 'Criminals Get Sun Tan At The Tax Payer's Expense.' On the smallest pretext the press go mad. I had to withdraw their privileges.

Another project we have input into is St Sampson's, a drop-in centre for the elderly. This was opened by the Queen Mother in 1974 but is still effective twenty years on. Originally it was partially funded by York Civic Trust and the York Round Table but has always relied on volunteers. It is especially useful to us because of the normality and also the pace of life. You are always on the go at Sampson's serving coffee, tea, soft drinks and light meals. It is so popular that people queue for seats. We work two or three days but even when prisoners are part-time there are real benefits. The building of relationships will always boost morale. The older end are especially good at nurturing a feeling of self-confidence in prisoners.

I suppose that one of the things a woman learns there is that no one has the word *prisoner* tattooed across their forehead. It is attractive to me because I feel that small group activity lets you into a normal world. Almost everybody who visits here says the same thing. They remark that the

Askham is primarily an education centre, for it draws people out and allows them time and space to explore their potential.

Tutor

Handing out cheques for charity, 1996

women seem pretty normal and most of them don't seem the least bit hard. Of course they are partly wrong; some are as hard as nails, but generally they are right. That is why you can afford to put faith in the Community Programme.

We have been running the scheme now for many years and it has been beneficial all round. As well as the Time Shop, the York Cemetery Project, the work with the RSPCA and St Sampson's, we are also doing work at the Yearsley Bridge Rehabilitation Centre, YACRO - the Yorkshire Association for the Care and Resettlement of Offenders - the Prince's Trust and the Greyhound Sanctuary in Selby.

I'm not sure if we can grow any further but this I do know; what we have achieved up to now has been impressive.

Stephanie Slater

BRANDED ON THE FOREHEAD

The first time I got into the train and travelled home I was really scared and unsure of myself. I felt that the word *prisoner* was branded across my forehead and that everybody knew who I was.

My home town is in the North East, everybody knows everybody, and my story had had good newspaper coverage but I was hardly a world class criminal. Still, I couldn't get it out of my mind that I was paying for my crime. One friend had stuck by me. She was unusual, my husband had gone in for a divorce and my family had disowned me, so that weekend staying with a friend was one on which I didn't do much. I clung to the house.

I was in a predicament. I wasn't eligible for the pre-release hostel for I wasn't a lifer coming to the end of my sentence but at Askham Grange

Before 1995 sentenced prisoners got their housing costs paid for up to 52 weeks which meant that many of them were able to retain their homes throughout their sentence. Following changes in the Housing Benefit rules of 1995 this period was cut to 13 weeks.

NACRO Report, 1995

there were alternatives. I might have done work in the house, the library was a possibility, but fortunately I got a chance to work in the Time Shop. It was the making of me. I was so scared when I got here but by the time I went on my next home visit I was prepared for life after prison. I relaxed and knew that the real problem was inside me. I didn't look a prisoner, that was in my imagination.

Looking back, I sometimes think that I did my real time in those thirteen months I waited until sentence was passed. That was when everything dropped apart. He left me and I came to feel very isolated. When I was sentenced I thought I knew what to expect. The first week alone in the cells was close to what I thought prison would be like. I was locked in, isolated, lonely and deserved to be. I hadn't anticipated Askham Grange or the realisation that people would be trying to help me to adjust.

I know I cannot go back to the work I did before and that I have to make do with other resources I have in me. Yet I also know there are other alternatives. I have always loved cooking and as the eldest of ten I am good at it. That gives me a start. I'm methodical, at times almost fussy, and I am organised. Although the Domestic Science room in Education has given me confidence, it has been the work in the Time Shop which has taught me that I am in with at least a sporting chance of survival as self-employed after prison is over.

Carol

Until they are risk-assessed prisoners need to be escorted; after a third of their sentence has been served they can go unescorted into the community to do voluntary work or for education.

Resettlement leave comes later.

Officer, 1997

THE REAL ME

The best of me comes out on home visits, not in here. In here you have to keep up your defences but when you are on the outside you can afford to relax. I was on a home visit and at a wedding the other week when a friend said to one of my friends, 'She's a real nice woman.' That's the real me.

I have been all over: Holloway, East Sutton Park, New Hall, and all the time I've wanted to improve myself. When I got here I wrote to all the colleges and eventually got on a fashion design course. I seem to have confidence but it is just confidence to deal with anything the prison can throw at me, not the confidence to deal with real life. After so many years I needed to be on the outside and test things out. I am coming to the end of my sentence, I will need time to adjust. The work in the shop is giving me a chance to adjust and contributing to helping me with my college work.

I am full-time at the college with a Saturday job at a big store in the centre of York. They offered me that when I went on a student visit, but it was the Time Shop in Upper Petergate which gave me my first chance to feel normal. It's a good name, Time Shop. We sell goods from prisons all over the country, anything from £400 doll's houses to knick-knacks at 50p. Hardly anyone senses that you are a prisoner. These days they are so used to charity shops that they think that you are a volunteer helper. It's strange, they even get to talking about how hard it must be to be a prisoner without having any idea that you are a prisoner yourself. One of the girls says, 'I'm doing life, I've already done eleven years,' - not me. When she says that I want to crawl under the counter and Lynne makes for the basement.

What the shop gives is a chance to return to normality. Of course you get skills like selling, stocktaking, mail order - we do a lot of mail order work - but it is the incidentals which matter as much as the vocational skills. You are on trust; and that's important too; probably more important than learning a trade or something which will get you a job. The phone is within reach but we know that we cannot use it. We also take money to the bank.

Sometimes as we sit in the little garden feeding the pigeons our sandwiches, I think how useful it has been to have been reintroduced to working life through something as pleasant as the Time Shop.

Prisoner

Every two months a prisoner can get up to five days' discretionary resettlement leave as long as she has an approved address. She might be going to find accommodation or employment. Most though would go to family.

Officer

A TRUST NEVER ABUSED 1947

The nearest Roman Catholic Church was at York. The Roman Catholic
women and I attended Mass at the Church of English Martyrs on Sundays.
During the first three months we trudged in the snow to the main road, and
travelled by bus to and from York. We were complete strangers; no one
knew who we were nor where we came from for some time. The news
leaked out eventually that we were the new occupants of Askham Grange.
At first, the women sat with me in the same pew in church, but as soon as
I felt I could trust them, they were allowed to sit where they liked. When
the service was over we all met outside the door, and returned home in the
same manner as other church-goers. The trust placed in them was never
abused. The women were always tidily dressed, and there was nothing in
their appearance or demeanour to distinguish them from anyone else in the
congregation. They were always provided with money for the church
collections. The Methodist and all the Non-Conformist women attended
Sunday evening service in the Methodist Hall in the village of Askham
Richard. At first a Methodist officer who wished to attend the service
accompanied them. Later, they were trusted to go by themselves. They
honoured this trust faithfully. One of them served as village organist for
approximately two years.

Mary Size

DOING A BUNK 1949

*The hardest thing about
Askham is that you can walk
out of this prison any time.*

Prisoner, 1997

'She was silly to steal the bicycle, though; when they get her she'll be up
on a new charge...' The breakfast tables were buzzing with the news. Jane,
sitting next to me, had known Munnings at Holloway... 'I don't know why
they ever sent her here,' she said, 'she's not the type ... She twice tried to

Medical staff, officers, prisoners and babies, 1971

commit suicide at Holloway, once by swallowing pins ... and the second time - well, you know how the long-timers are allowed to plant a few things in a plot there if they want to? She asked for poppies, swallowed the seeds, and was asleep for a week. The Governor must have known the sort she was - Munnings was serving a sentence at Aylesbury when she was Gov there ... Maybe she thought she could reform her ... Pity, we don't want escapes from here ... It'll mean they'll tighten up the rules for the rest of us ... you'll see.' It was a strange atmosphere. At Holloway everybody would have wished 'good luck' to an escaped prisoner. At Askham it was considered that she had let the old school down; it was like shooting at a sitting bird - too easy. Blackett, Munnings' room-mate, did not appear. It was reported that she had spent the morning being questioned. It was generally supposed that she would be sent away. The workroom that morning buzzed with speculation. Cars kept coming up the drive with the local police and press. The Governor appeared at mid-morning looking pale and grave. The excitement prevailed for several days. Blackett was still with us. She had sworn that she knew nothing about it. Eventually it came out that Munnings had got back to London, having sold the bicycle for the fare. She had then rung up the Governor of Holloway and asked if she could go back there, as she didn't like it at Askham.

Jean Henry

A VERY IMPORTANT PERSON 1992

Dear Mr Crew

I'll start from the beginning. At the airport I had to wait two hours until I was allowed to enter the plane. The immigrations officers were ok and as I walked around with an attitude of a Very Important Person nobody knew that I

If someone absconds you need to put them somewhere. We have a small unit with locked cells. If one cell is used once a month that's as much as it is.

Harry Crew

Barbecue, 1996

was a prisoner and was treated with regards due to a VIP. The flight seemed to be a trip to fairyland, red sunset above a field of snow-white clouds with sudden patches of clouds that - with some imagination - could have been a mountain landscape, inhabited by giants, monsters and huge animals.

Flying always gives me a thrill. I love the sensation of power when the plane takes off. The sky was clear above Holland and I could see the rimshaped agglomeration of cities down below like a chain of diamonds.

Nobody bothered me, no police, no customs.

My passport had been marked with a deportation notice, so I conveniently forgot to take it out of my pocket when I washed my jeans in the washing machine at a high-temperature programme. The remnants I'll take to the City Council to swap for a nice clean European passport. Problem? No.

It still feels as if a bond has been cut. I never really felt like a foreigner and I was very close to several people in prison as well as outside. Your sympathy and friendship helped me to cope with the years that I was separated from my family and friends and I sincerely thank you for that.

Wilma

Outside I had a five-bedroomed house, everything as I wanted it, and two fellas on the go. I had a lifestyle. When I get out of here I'll be homeless.

Prisoner, 1996

GREAT EXPECTATIONS *1950*

The day before I left Askham was a Sunday, so it was arranged that my farewell party was to be held on the Saturday afternoon. There were only to be about seven or eight, including Kate and myself. We had asked permission to have it in our little room, and we planned to light a fire in the afternoon and make everything as cosy as possible. Miss Jackson allowed Kate and me to go to the village shop after lunch and buy some extra cakes with the money we had; she herself contributed some cigarettes, which we thought was very kind of her. We strolled out of the gates in our most nonchalant manner. Of course all the villagers and the people in the shops knew we were prisoners, dressed as we were in our blue cotton dresses and dark serge cloaks, but they had become used to seeing us. I thought of Monday morning when I should drive through the gates never to return. 'Give me the chair. I want to look on top of the cupboard to see what I've got left in the way of soap and bath cubes. You can have most of it, but there's one or two people I want to give something to. Look, David has sent me some cigarettes for the journey.' Kate stretched herself on the bed. 'I can see you amid clouds of smoke in the restaurant-car knocking back brandies and sodas and dropping envelopes with HM Prison, Holloway, all over the place for respectable passengers with eyes on stalks to pick up.' - 'Poppy is going to meet me at King's Cross. I've said that I don't want to see David until the evening, when I've had time to tart myself up a bit.' - 'Well, I hope you're still standing by the evening.' - 'I wonder what a drink will taste like after eight months? Oh, to sleep on a soft bed again, and have a proper pillow...and wear nylons...and soak myself in scent!... Oh, Kate, I mustn't go on like this: it's hateful of me.'

Jean Henry

SOME CRITICISMS 1994

I realise that most establishments do not provide the Home Leave and Open Visits that Askham Grange allowed when I was in custody, and I was very grateful for the time that I got to spend with my family whilst I was

The more ways that can be found to consult prisoners about the organisation and the delivery of the regime, the more likely it is that their needs and concerns can be met without resort to formal complaints procedures.

Home Office Report, 1996

serving my sentence but I found the Prison Service unsympathetic towards my situation. I was sentenced in Portsmouth, and went to Holloway, then Cookham Wood. Although I was relieved to be transferred from both these prisons, Askham was so far away from home. It proved difficult for my family and friends to visit me, as the distance and expense was so great. I was granted an extra night on the three occasions that I went on home leave, which I was very grateful for - but once I was accepted onto the hostel I found that I was refused any extra time to allow for travelling - even with work permitting. The University of York were very sympathetic towards my situation and often offered me extra days off to enable me to go home - but for one reason or another the Prison refused. It seemed that there was one rule for one person and another rule for another. Because of this I rarely took advantage of the home leave rule. Inmates should be given allowances if they are placed at such a distance from their family. I was lucky because my mum was prepared to travel any distance to see me, but not all people are as lucky - and they could find themselves doing a lengthy sentence without visits or Home Leave. I initially transferred to Askham on the understanding that I would be transferred to East Sutton Park shortly after, but on my arrival at Askham was told that I had 'no chance' of getting moved nearer to my home.

Askham Grange is definitely in a league of its own. It seems genuinely committed to rehabilitation and aiding and supporting the inmate, as opposed to punishing. I am grateful to have been given the opportunity to serve my sentence at Askham Grange; if only more prisons operated the same regime then I am sure that re-offending would be reduced, and prisoners would leave custody with a better attitude, as well as with useful new skills and the knowledge that they have achieved something, as opposed to spending 23 hours a day locked in a cell.

Emma

Governors of open prisons may wish to consider temporary release for a mother to attend birthday parties and special family occasions or to visit a sick child. It may even be appropriate to consider temporary release for parents' evenings when the distances are not great.

Home Office,
Regimes For Women, 1994

(This now no longer the case due to changes in temporary release rules.)

GOODBYE GOVERNOR 1950

Sunday was a cold, bright October day. I did the room out very thoroughly while Kate was with the chickens. I had to hand in all my prison clothes to be checked that afternoon. I had asked for permission to take out my paint-box, as it was rather a good one; as a rule anything that was sent to you became prison property when you left. Any correspondence that you wanted to take with you would also have to be handed in to be re-censored in case you had added any messages or addresses. I was formally discharged by the Governor in the presence of an officer early that afternoon.

On the day of discharge, the prisoner is officially free at four o'clock that afternoon, but I don't think it would have met with approval if I had insisted on taking the night train. I was due to leave York at nine the next morning and arrive in London just after one. The chaplain was nice and friendly. As I left the office I ran into the Governor, and she drew me into her study. 'Goodbye, Jean. Let me know how you get on.' - 'Goodbye, madam, and thank you. In some ways I think I am quite sorry to say that I am afraid I shan't see you again.' I paused. Had I gone too far? I need not have worried. The Governor laughed. Her face was rather stern in repose, but when she laughed she really laughed. It bubbled up from somewhere inside, and her eyes twinkled, so that her face was at once transformed. 'Goodbye, my child. Good luck and God bless you.' She held out her hand, and I gripped it. 'Goodbye, madam,' I repeated, and fled out of the room. As I went, I wondered how far the experiment of a women's prison-without-bars in this country would owe its success in the future to its first Governor.

Jean Henry

Just after Christmas a young woman who had been unhappy here decided to abscond. When we caught her in the middle of a field she asked, 'How did you know which way I went?' - 'Not difficult, love, there's three inches of snow and you are wearing red trousers.'

Officer

Leaving A Friend 1950

Kate's black head was still buried in the pillow when I awoke the following morning. I got out of bed very quietly, so as not to disturb her. I put on my dressing-gown and slippers, and, taking my prison garments off the chair, went along to the bathroom. The water was hot, but usually there was no time to have a bath at this hour. I put a bath cube in the water, one I had saved for the purpose. I was nearly dressed when the bell went. When I got back to our room Kate had gone. I rolled up my bedding. My inside felt all funny and shaky, and I sat down on the bed to put on my shoes. Kate reappeared. 'I'll send you a postcard and things ... it won't be long,' I said. She sat down on her unmade bed and covered her face with her hands. Her thin body shook with sobs. I had never seen her cry before. I put my arms round her. 'Don't ... Please don't ... I must go ... Come to the window if you can.' I went out of the room, carrying my roll of bedding. I met one or two prisoners on the stairs. They wished me good luck. I stood outside the office door. Soon Miss Jackson appeared and I went in with her. She had my bag. She went through its contents, checking them with the list in front of her. She gave me a railway pass. Then we went to the property room, where all the prisoner's clothes are on hangers, with the owner's name written on a card attached to them, and their shoes neatly stowed away in boxes. She saw that I was agitated. 'It's Kate,' I said, 'I hate her being so upset.' - 'It's natural, lass,' she said kindly. 'You've been together a long time.' I took off my clothes in front of her, all except my suspender belt and brassiere, which were my own. 'Do you want to examine these?' I said. 'No, that's all right; put your things on.' She handed me my own clothes. 'You'll catch your death in those flimsies,' she added, 'after the underclothes you've been used to.'

Jean Henry

Every year several hundred prisoners pass through this prison. Some make friends for life but others have what they call 'prison friends'.

But still a prison

THE DUCK GIRL 1967 - 1996

Nowadays Askham Grange doesn't have a prisoner called the 'Duck Girl' to look after the ducks on the pond but when I joined the Prison Service here in 1967, they did. At that time she was a woman in her forties who was serving a life sentence for murder. I never knew the details of her crime, but as I was a sprog officer and had never met anyone like her before, I brought my prejudices from the outside with me. She had made a deep impression on me, with no effort on her part, and I was rather in awe of her.

When I returned to Askham 26 years later, I had changed quite a lot though Askham itself was in many ways unchanged. Structurally, there were quite a few changes - the black and white stairs had been carpeted, an Education Department and Works Department and new Prisoners' Dining Room had all been built, and the officers no longer lived in the house. However, in many ways, the atmosphere of caring and the traditions of helping prisoners with their rehabilitation into society, although developed by modern resources, were unchanged. The major changes were in me. I had returned to Askham with much experience of the Service and of life, and to perform a different role - that of Deputy Governor.

Experienced prison staff do not think of prisoners in terms of their offences before any other considerations. We need to know about offences, in order to help individual people, and to steer them in the direction of appropriate courses: Anger Management Course, Assertiveness Courses, or Drug or Alcohol Abuse Counselling for instance, but we tend to look at the whole person, and assess prisoners more on character, and behaviour, and we consider how the resources of the prison can best be used to help them.

I have observed that people with little or no knowledge of prisoners who visit prisons, often have at the forefront of their minds the question 'what

Some of us on the outside remember the pain of being inside at Christmas.

For those of you due out in 1997 it's just around the corner, for those of you with no date yet, remember, only your body can be imprisoned, never your mind.

God bless you.

Merry Christmas and hoping that 1997 brings your dreams into reality.

Card from a former prisoner

crime has he or she committed?' and this can sometimes be a barrier to communication. Whilst never encouraging this, I understand it - that was how I felt all those years ago about the Duck Girl.

Margaret Middlemiss

A Letter To Mrs Rhodes

Things between Steve and I came to a head in June. He had become withdrawn, hardly speaking to me and showed no interest in what I was doing and I became very angry. I even considered starting a life on my own but I knew that I really wanted to sort things out. I therefore told him how unhappy I was and that I was thinking about a separation; something I would never have done before all this happened. He was really shocked and over a week we did a lot of talking and crying. When I had come home he said it sounded as if I had been on holiday; as you said, people block out the worse memories. So I told him all the low points which was difficult for me, as I had buried them, but I recognised I had to get it all out of my system. Anyway, we were able to sort all our feelings out and we are like a couple of newlyweds!! He is affectionate and very protective of me which is what I have always wanted. We discuss everything and he is so proud of what I have achieved since March. I feel the past has now been laid to rest and I can get on planning my future.

Prisoner

Dear Mr Crew

Thanks for persuading Home Office to get rid of me 'one whole week' earlier. I'll sign this card (last one I didn't) haha!

Best wishes

Maggie

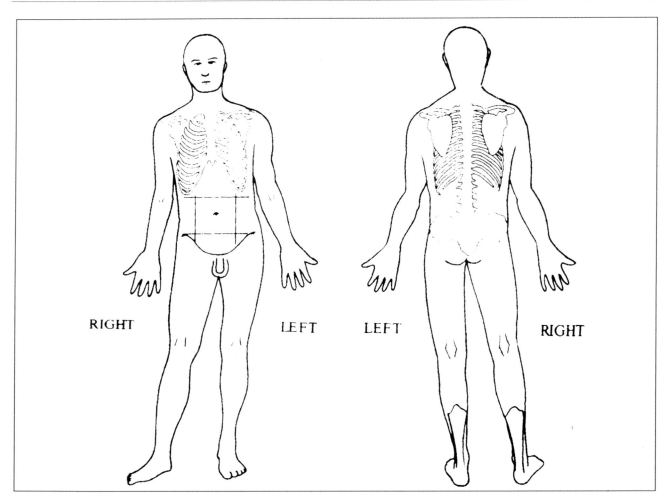

RIGHT   LEFT   LEFT   RIGHT

Diagram used by doctors in women's prisons up to the present

THE MISSING BITS

I sometimes think this diagram says it all. It doesn't come from the dim and distant past, it is still in use. If a prison doctor needed to locate the source of pain or the position of an injury this is the diagram that is actually used in all prisons, including women's prisons. They must have spent a lot of time looking for the missing bits.

It's easy to joke but it illustrates the point made by Helena Kennedy in her foreword:

> *In a system designed essentially for men, women can reap*
> *the consequences of inadequate provision, unsuitable to*
> *their needs.*

It is often against the odds that a Prison Service originally set up and developed with male offenders in mind manages to meet the needs of women in prison. At its best, as in Askham Grange, and with staff dedicated to rehabilitation, the service succeeds in making a constructive contribution to the way our society deals with crime and punishment.

Reini Schühle